Painting on SILK

Painting on SILK

Jill Kennedy & Jane Varrall

Dryad Press Ltd London

Acknowledgment

We would like to thank our husbands and our families for
their support and encouragement, and our friends for their
help and enthusiasm, especially Lily for typing, Sarah for
reading, Karen for fixing and I. Zone.

Photographs taken by J. P. Van Den Waeyenberg
              Fotostudio Jean-Pierre
              Mechelsesteenweg 232
              1960 Sterrebeek
              Belgium

ISBN 0-85219-752-7

Typeset by Servis Filmsetting Ltd, Manchester
and printed in Great Britain by
Jolly & Barber Ltd, Rugby
and bound by Anchor Brendon Ltd, Tiptree
for the publishers
Dryad Press Ltd
8 Cavendish Square
London W1M 0AJ

Kennedy, J. (Jill).
  Painting on silk.
  1. Silk. Painting – Manuals
  I. Title II. Varrall, J. (Jane)
  746.6

Contents

Introduction

For centuries the rich texture and lustre of silk have made it one of the most valued of fabrics. This book aims to help you create your own designs on this sought-after material. Silk painting is a relatively new and expanding art form, simple but versatile, which exploits both the natural qualities of the fabric and the artistic opportunities presented by modern permanent silk-painting dyes.

The book is divided into three sections. The first is a comprehensive introduction to the equipment and material needed for techniques explained in the book, with up-to-date information on the available products.

The middle section introduces techniques step-by-step, illustrated with diagrams and photographs. The samples and articles in the photographs have been specially painted for the book by the authors. Despite the great variety of interesting and exciting methods of painting on silk, even beginners with no previous experience of silk painting should be able to understand the techniques in this section and produce their own rewarding work, while the more experienced silk painter will be introduced to advanced and innovative ways of using this art form.

The final section includes photographs of and information on completed projects. These are of course only suggestions, as silk paintings can be used to create all sorts of different articles, from pictures, cards, cushions and lampshades, to scarves, ties and clothes. It can provide enormous scope for engaging your own imagination and artistry.

Part one

Equipment

Fig. 1 Silk, pongée 9

1

Silk

Silk is a superb fabric to work with, and can be used for all of the painting techniques described in this book. It has a natural lustre and gloss which mean that it has beautiful decorative properties. Its chief characteristics are strength, warmth without weight, resistance to creasing and comfort when worn.

History

The silk industry was first established in China in 2640 BC, and gradually spread throughout Asia and India and west to Persia. Silk became prized as a royal cloth and in medieval times Spain, Italy and France were famous for their silks. In England the use of silk was widespread among the nobility by the time of Elizabeth I. Charles II brought many skilled French weavers to England and in 1718 the first spinning mill began to operate in Derby. Attempts to start the industry in America were, however, unsuccessful.

Origin

Today, about 60% of the world's raw silk is produced in Japan. China is the next largest producer, followed by India and Pakistan. The industry is called *Sericulture*, which is the large-scale rearing of cultivated silk worms. These are the larvae of *Bombix mori*, the silk moths which feed on mulberry leaves. The silk thread is obtained by reeling off the double filaments from the cocoons formed when the larvae pupate. The silk filament this produces is fine and uniformly smooth.

The caterpillars of wild silk moths, such as tussah, feed in the open on leaves of various trees, including a type of oak. The silk these produce is frequently irregular, and when woven produces the *slub*, or variation of thickness, which is the chief characteristic of wild silk.

Different Types

Like other fibres, silk can be woven in various ways to produce fabric of different types and textures. Woven silk can be embellished by introducing a pattern in the course of weaving. Woven silks are available in different widths: 80, 90, 115, 120 and 140 cm. The following types of silk can all be used for the techniques described in this book:

pongée No. 5 – No. 10
twill
wild silk
crêpe de chine
brocade
chiffon
douppion
satin
shantung
tussah
organza

Fig. 2 Pongée 9

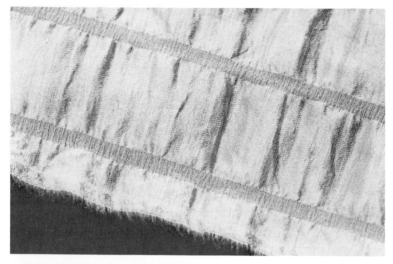

Fig. 3 Cloqué

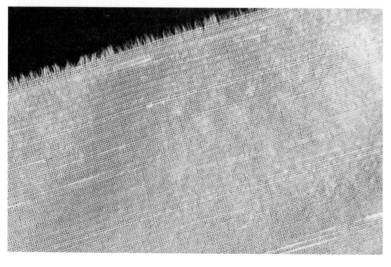

Fig. 4 Wild silk

Fig. 5 Twill

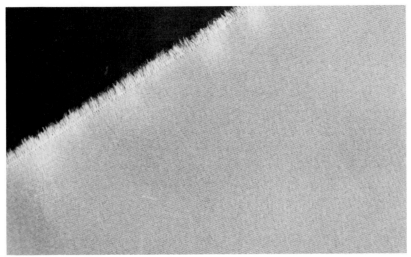

Fig. 6 Satin

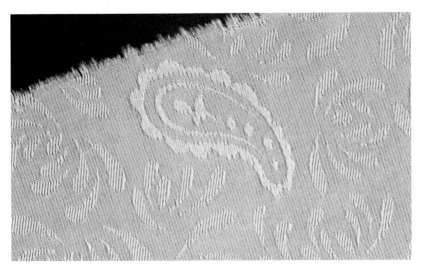

Fig. 7 Brocade

11

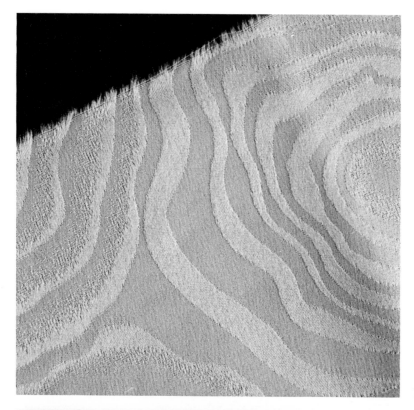

Fig. 8 Brocade

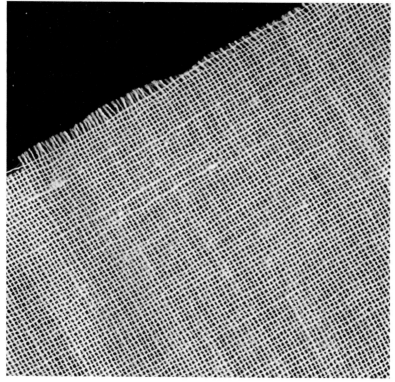

Fig. 9 Wool

Pongée

Pongée is smooth and shiny and ideal for silk painting. This silk is chiefly used for linings and may be found in your department store under the name of *Habutai* or Jap silk. It is a soft plain-weave fabric which is sold in a variety of thicknesses, from No. 5 to No. 10. The higher the number, the thicker the silk. When painting on a thinner fabric, less dye is needed. Choose a natural-coloured silk, such as white or off-white.

We recommend that beginners use pongée at first, as it is relatively cheap and works well for all the techniques.

Uses: No. 5 – experimental techniques, scarves, pictures, cards
No. 9 – scarves, lampshades, blouses, pictures, experimental techniques, cards
No. 10 – cushions, ties, blouses, dresses, skirts.

Pongée Clocqué

A plain woven silk with ruched bands.

Uses: t-shirts, blouses, dresses.

Wild Silk

Wild silk is woven from the silk filaments of the wild Tussah moth. This fabric is sometimes known as raw, or Tussore, silk. It is a thicker fabric than that from cultivated moths and the slubs or irregularities can cause problems when using the serti technique. The texture of the fabric must be considered when designing and choosing a project.

Uses: scarves, cushions, ties, skirts, t-shirts, blouses, jackets, trousers, screens.

Twill

This is a fabric with a diagonal rib produced in the weaving. The twill weave gives silk more sheen.

Uses: cushions, ties, clothing, scarves.

Crêpe de Chine

A lightweight plain-weave fabric composed of highly twisted yarns which shrink in different directions during finishing, producing a characteristic surface texture.

Uses: this fabric drapes and hangs well. We recommend it for clothes and exclusive scarves.

Satin

A type of weave in which the warp predominates over the weft, giving a characteristic smooth, lustrous surface. Duchess satin has a rich feel, and lingerie satin made from crêpe yarns is supple and soft.

Uses: lingerie, clothes.

Brocade

A self-coloured pattern woven on a special loom. Many interesting designs are available. The paisley and tree bark are shown in Figs. 7 and 8.

Uses: blouses, dresses, lingerie, ties.

Wool

It is possible to use a very fine wool with silk-painting dyes.

Uses: scarves, ties, clothes.

Care of Your Silk

To clean silk, wash it gently without rubbing in tepid, soapy water. Harsh detergent must not be used, as it will cause the colour to fade. Rinse thoroughly in warm water and roll in a tea-towel to remove excess moisture. Press on the wrong side with a steam iron or use a damp cloth.

Some silks may have had an application of size or dressing to increase their weight. Before painting, wash the silk out thoroughly in warm soapy water. The dyes will then penetrate evenly and thoroughly.

Fig. 10 A selection of frames

2

Frames

A wooden frame is an essential piece of equipment when painting on silk. The fabric must be raised above the work-surface, and so it is necessary for it to be stretched over a rigid frame. If the silk is not raised and stretched, it is impossible to paint the design correctly. There are several types of frame available.

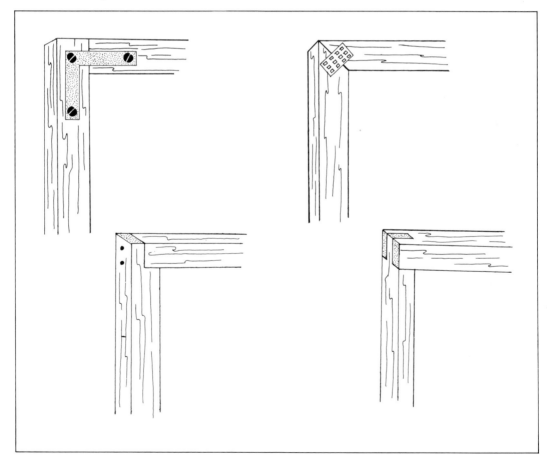

Fig. 11 Corner construction of a fixed wooden frame

Fixed Wooden Frame

These frames are the easiest to make. The wood used must be a white softwood of approximately 2 cm × 3 cm. The frame must lie flat on the work surface, so it must be made rigid and even. The major disadvantage of a fixed frame is that the size cannot be adjusted. An old wooden picture frame can be used.

To construct a fixed wooden frame, cut four lengths of wood to the required size. These can then be assembled in one of the following ways:

a. a simple butt joint with metal angle bracket

b. a simple butt joint with screw

c. a mitred joint with glue and staples.

Adjustable Wooden Slot-Frame

The adjustable wooden slot-frame can be used for various sizes of fabric. We have found that a softwood frame which accommodates a 90 cm × 90 cm width fabric is the most useful. Slots are cut at regular intervals down each side of the frame, enabling the four lengths of wood to form different-sized squares or rectangles when fitted together in different ways. Accurate cutting of the slots will ensure a good, tight-fitting frame.

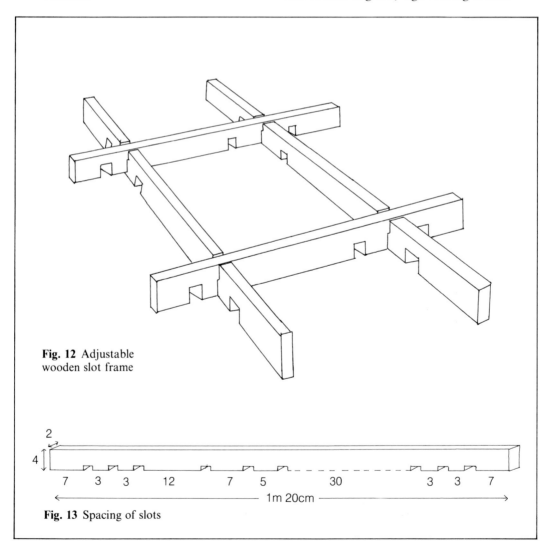

Fig. 12 Adjustable wooden slot frame

2
4
7   3   3   12   7   5   30   3   3   7
←———————— 1m 20cm ————————→

Fig. 13 Spacing of slots

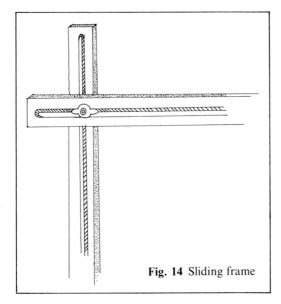

Fig. 14 Sliding frame

Sliding Frames

These are made of four lengths of wood or metal with four wing-nuts to keep the frame rigid. On wooden frames the silk is pinned on to two opposite sides of the frame, then pulled taut and the frame fastened with the wing-nuts. A more expensive sliding wooden frame is available, which has a row of small picot pins protruding from the wooden slat. Care must be taken when pushing the silk on to these pins, as they are very sharp. The most expensive sliding frames are made of metal and use magnets to hold the silk in place. The advantage of this frame is no pin-marks are made on the silk, and it can be tightened without being unfastened.

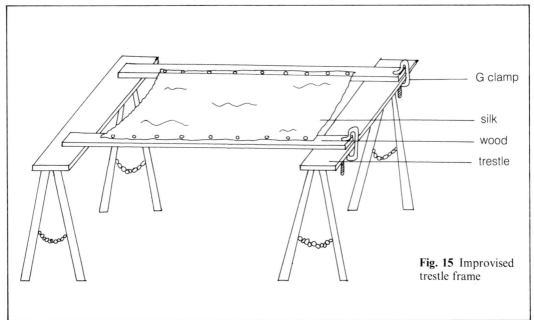

G clamp

silk

wood

trestle

Fig. 15 Improvised trestle frame

Improvised Frames for Larger Pieces of Work

When working with a large piece of silk which needs to be painted in one piece, for example a sarong, large wall-hanging or piece of clothing, it is a good idea to improvise a frame specially. Here are two suggestions:

a. Cut two pieces of softwood 10 cm longer than your silk. Position two trestles and place a plank of wood on each end. Secure the lengths of wood firmly on top of the planks with either G-clamps or strong tape.

b. Place two adjustable slot-frames end to end and either bind with tape or fix together firmly using card and staples.

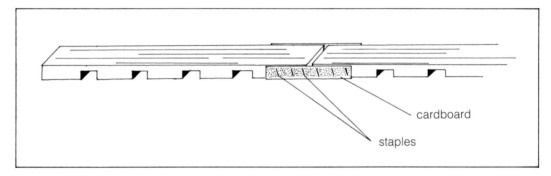

Fig. 16 Improvised slot frame

Fig. 17 Types of pin

Pins

Unless you have a magnetic metal frame, you need to use special fine-pointed pins so that the silk is not torn when it is secured to the frame. Architect's pins are ideal because they have three small points to hold the silk firmly and can be removed easily using a small lever. If these are not available, look for push-pins or drawing-pins with a long, fine point.

Stretching the Silk on to the Frame

To achieve a successful design, even and taut stretching of the silk is essential.

Work can often be spoilt by a dye-stained frame, so we suggest that the frame be protected with strips of masking tape before the silk is stretched. This tape can be easily removed and renewed before each new project.

Adjust the frame to the required size and cut or tear the silk to fit its outside dimensions. Place the silk design uppermost over the frame, and begin pinning along one side. Stretch the silk using the grain of the fabric as a guide, placing a pin every 3 cm. Continue along the adjacent side and then pin the remaining sides. When you have finished pinning, the silk should be tight and firm like a drum.

If the piece of silk you have is too small for your frame, it is possible to make it fit by using dressmaking pins and long strips of fabric. Secure two sides firmly and attach tape as shown in Fig. 21.

Alternatively, a small piece of silk could be stretched on to an embroidery hoop.

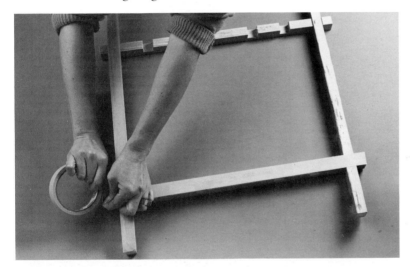

Fig. 18 Frame being masked with masking tape

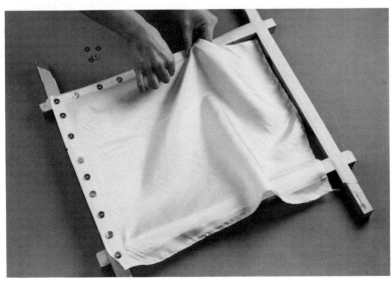

Fig. 19 Silk being stretched on to frame

Fig. 20 Firmly stretched
silk

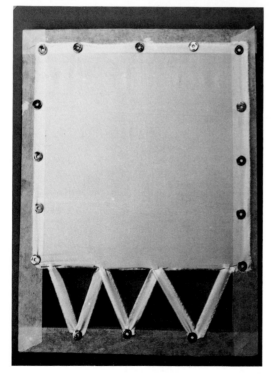

Fig. 21 Tape method of
attaching silk to frame

Fig. 22 Silk in
embroidery hoop

3
Brushes

There are many types of brush available, but initially three or four brushes of different sizes should be adequate. The brushes are numbered – the lower the number, the finer the tip. It pays to buy the best quality you can afford, as a good brush will last.

Silk-Painting Brushes

Wash brushes are ideal for silk painting as they have a fine point and spring back into shape after each brushstroke. Depending on their size, they are able to hold enough dye to cover quite large areas. We suggest sable, or, if you are prepared to make an investment, the silk-painting wash brushes, with their wooden handles and coil attachment of hairs. These brushes, especially the medium-thick end of the range, have the capacity to hold a large reservoir of dye and thus facilitate smooth painting. As the popularity of silk painting has increased, a special cheaper silk-painting brush has been introduced. For finer work, Chinese bamboo brushes are acceptable. Ox-hair and squirrel-hair brushes can be used, but will need replacing after several months of constant use.

Care of Silk-Painting Brushes

Silk-painting brushes are expensive, so be sure to look after them. After use, rinse thoroughly, ensuring that all dye has been removed from the base. Extra care must be taken with the thick wash-brushes. It may even be necessary to wash the brush in warm soapy water to completely remove the darker dyes, otherwise your next piece of work could be ruined.

After washing, rinse your brush carefully in clean water, reshape it and leave it to dry, bristles uppermost. Special brush-holders are available: these suspend the brush by a metal coil, leaving the tips undamaged. Never leave the brushes standing in water or seal them away in an airtight container.

Wax Brushes

Quality is not as important a consideration when choosing brushes to be used with a wax technique. The constant heat of the melted wax tends to shorten the life of any brush. Flat-headed bristle brushes are ideal and even an old one-inch or two-inch household painting brush can be used to cover background areas easily. A finer sable brush can be kept for delicate, intricate work. It is possible to work with one medium-sized brush which can be trimmed to a wedge, so that the point can be used for waxing very fine lines.

Care of Wax Brushes

Cleaning brushes which are coated in wax is difficult. They can be cleaned in white spirit

Fig. 23 A selection of
brushes

or hot water to melt the wax so that it floats off. This can be a laborious task, so we suggest you set aside brushes to be used solely for wax techniques, eliminating the need for cleaning them.

Stencil Brushes

These are inexpensive and can be obtained in a variety of sizes. They are short-handled with round, flat tips. Any stiff bristle brush may be used, however, if the bristles are cut down to make it more rigid.

Alternatives to Brushes

Cotton wool can be used to make alternatives to brushes. A large, firm cotton-wool ball can be attached to a stick with wire or masking tape to make an ideal applicator for large background areas. For smaller areas, a tight ball of cotton wool secured in a clothes peg can be used (make-up removal pads are just right for this purpose). Cotton buds are very useful for small areas.

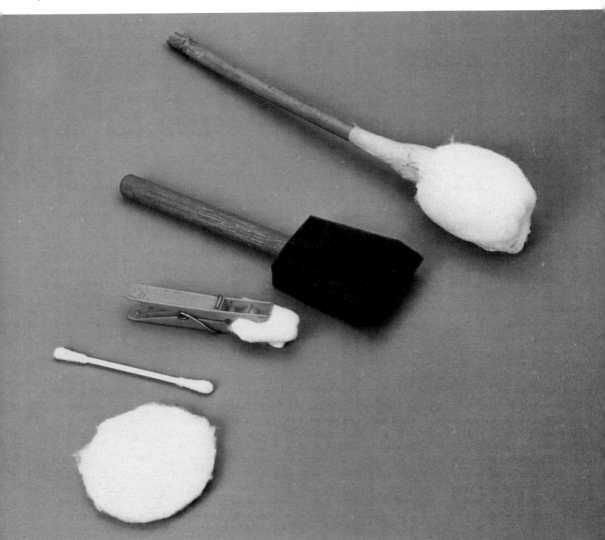

Fig. 24 Alternatives to brushes

23

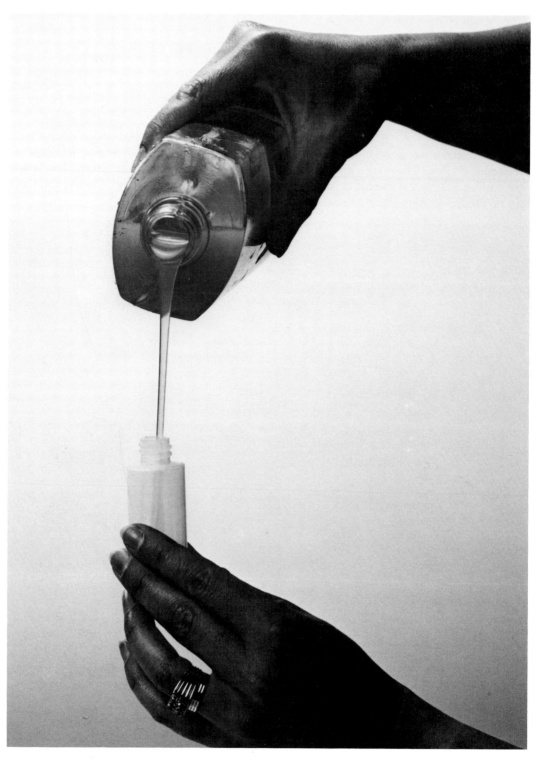

Fig. 25 Filling the
pipette

4

Gutta

Gutta is a white rubber liquid. Gutta-percha (its full name) is obtained from trees belonging to the *Sapotacea* family which are natives of Malaya, Borneo and Sumatra. These trees are now grown on plantations and are hybrids of species of *Palaquium*. The mature leaves are gathered and ground in mills to free the fibres from the gutta-percha. The mass is then soaked in water for about thirty minutes, which waterlogs the leaf tissue,

Fig. 26 Flower with and without gutta barrier

then plunged into cold water so that the gutta percha floats to the surface, where it is collected. The gutta percha is also tapped from the trees. The latex is coagulated by hot water and the gutta-percha recovered. Once cleaned, it is formed into blocks for sale.

The gutta available in specialist art and craft shops is a thick colourless liquid which has the consistency of syrup. After the gutta has been applied to the silk it remains soft and pliable, even when dry. The purpose of the gutta line is to penetrate the fibre of the silk to create a barrier which is waterproof, and therefore dyeproof. When dye is painted on silk it will naturally flow and spread along the warp and weft of the fabric. The fine lines of gutta prevent the dye from spreading, thus enabling a controlled design to be painted. The colour of the silk will show through these lines which remain undyed.

Preparation of Gutta

Correct consistency of the gutta is vital for successful results. If the gutta is too thick, it sits on the surface of the fabric and does not penetrate the fibres of the silk. Conversely, if it is too thin, the barrier will not be waterproof or dyeproof.

When you buy gutta it is normally in bottles or tins, ready for use. There are three types available, one of which is water-based. Sometimes gutta thickens with age, especially when left in contact with the air, so make sure the bottle is tightly sealed when not in use. It is possible to thin down the gutta, if it has become thick and sticky, by using one of several thinning agents on the market, essence F (diluent for gutta), white spirit and water. It is important to check which thinner is needed with your brand of gutta.

Always do a sample test with your gutta and dye before use to check that it is the correct consistency. A gutta which is too thick needs the thinner added one drop at a time and should be shaken until the right consistency is achieved. This takes practice: after a while a workable gutta will be easily recognised.

Coloured and Metallic Guttas

In certain pieces of work a white outline may be rather limiting. It is possible to use coloured and metallic guttas to liven up your work.

Coloured gutta is usually sold in small quantities and is therefore more expensive than the colourless type. It is possible to make your own, however, by adding either stained glass colour or typographic ink to ordinary gutta. To prepare this gutta mix a small amount of the colour with the thinning agent (essence F and white spirit), and then add to the colourless gutta. Shake thoroughly before use.

Metallic gutta is also sold in small quantities and is very expensive. It can create a lovely effect, but is more difficult to work with because it is more liquid and the metallic particles tend to clog. We recommend that beginners work with the colourless gutta until the technique has been mastered.

Coloured and metallic guttas should not be dry cleaned as the colour dissolves. Wash the fabric in warm soapy water.

Containers for the Application of Gutta

To apply the gutta to the silk a pipette or cone is needed. We suggest that beginners use a pipette, as although a fine line can be achieved with a cone it can be very difficult to manipulate.

The pipette is a small plastic bottle with a screw top and a spout. Remove these, then carefully and slowly pour the prepared gutta into the bottle until it is three-quarters full. If you find this difficult, insert a small funnel into the pipette, or squeeze the pipette to express the air and then draw in the gutta.

A decision must now be made about the thickness of the outline required.

The plastic spout can be pierced with a fine needle to produce a gutta line, but you may prefer to affix a nomographic nib which enables you to regulate the flow of the gutta, producing a perfect, even line. These nibs are available in different sizes from No. 4 – No. 9

Fig. 27 Pipette and nibs

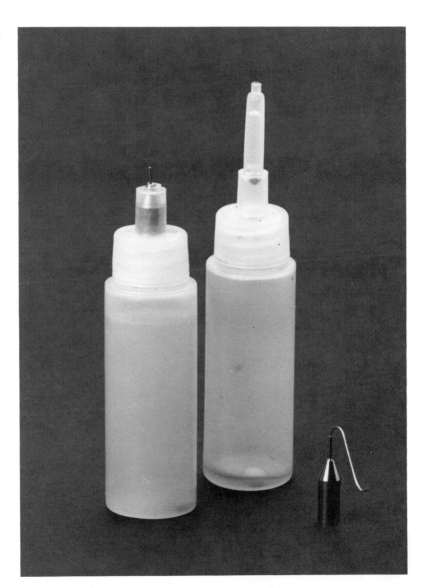

Fig. 28 Gutta lines of different widths

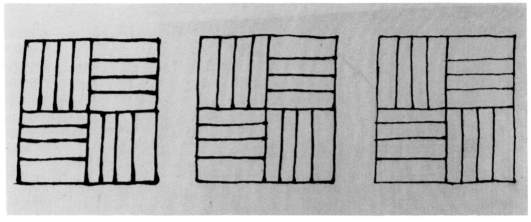

(the lower the number, the finer the hole). We suggest a No. 5 unless a very thick line is required, when a No. 9 should be used.

The nib should be secured either by attaching it firmly to the spout with tape or by cutting off the spout and placing it inside the screw-on cap. The nib comes supplied with a fine wire which should be kept as it may be useful to unblock the hole. To keep the nibs ready for use, they should be placed in a small airtight container of thinning fluid (essence F, white spirit or water).

Make sure you use the gutta within a few hours, otherwise evaporation will spoil its consistency. Never leave gutta in your pipette overnight or it will harden. Always drain the remaining gutta back into the original container.

Fig. 29 Use of home-made cone

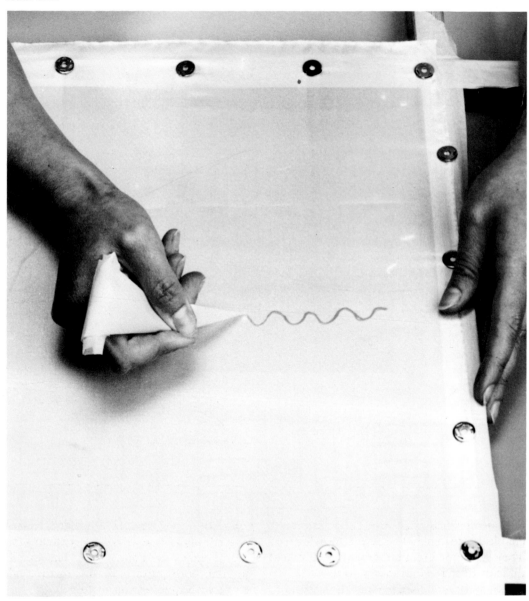

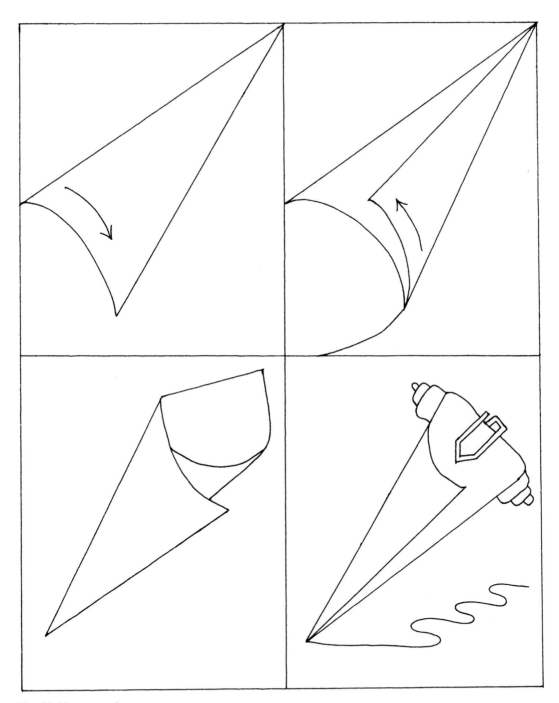

Fig. 30 How to make a cone

Many professionals use cones, as these enable an extremely fine line to be achieved. They are not popular because they are difficult to make and messy to use.

To make your own cone, greaseproof, waxed or tracing paper is needed. Cut a rectangle of paper approximately 20 cm × 16 cm and make a cone as shown in Fig. 30. Fill the cone with gutta and roll up the end. Secure with a paper-clip or tape.

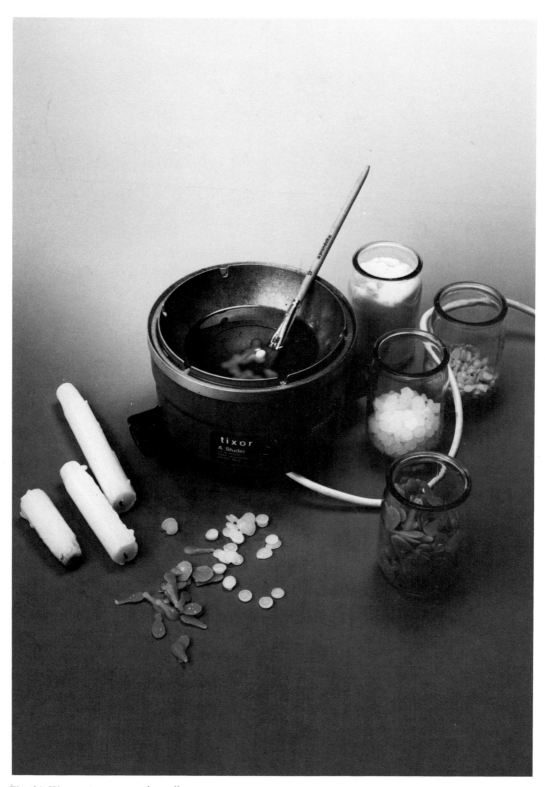

Fig. 31 Wax pot, waxes and candles

5

Wax

Wax can be used in the same way as gutta in the dyeing process. When applied to the silk, hot wax creates a barrier by penetrating the silk fibres, and so areas that have been covered with liquid wax will remain undyed. This process of applying molten wax and dyes is traditionally known as batik. This is usually a long process which involves immersing the silk completely in a dye bath. This book will cover a simpler 'batik' technique called 'false batik'.

Types of Wax

The wax is a mixture of paraffin wax and beeswax. Paraffin wax is white in colour and can be bought as candles, blocks, powder or in beads. It is easily obtained from hardware stores, craft shops or candlemakers' suppliers. The beeswax is more expensive than the paraffin wax and is yellow in colour, but this does not affect the silk. Beeswax is harder to find but is available at specialist craft shops and candlemakers' suppliers.

Preparation of Wax

Paraffin wax could be used alone, but when dry it is extremely brittle and has a tendency to peel off the silk. If this happens, the barrier created by the wax will not be dyeproof and your work may be spoiled. The addition of beeswax to the paraffin wax makes a more malleable blend which will not peel so easily.

We suggest that when mixing the waxes you use six parts paraffin wax to four parts beeswax. This will produce a good mix for line work. Depending on the required end result, these quantities can be varied. Heavier crackle will be obtained by increasing the ratio of paraffin wax. A smooth, plain area can be obtained by using beeswax only. A ready-prepared 'batik wax' is also available in granulated form, and is ideal for this technique.

Heating of Wax

The wax must be heated slowly. This may be done by one of the following methods: thermostatically-controlled wax-pot; electric ring with saucepan, double boiler or aluminium tin; thermostatically-controlled frying-pan; gas burner or camping gas stove with saucepan, double boiler or tin.

Wax and its fumes are highly inflammable and extreme care must be taken not to overheat it. For this reason we recommend the thermostatically-controlled wax-pot, as this can keep the wax at a constant temperature of 250°F (120°C). Unless you intend to use wax frequently, this wax-pot is an expensive item and the wax can be heated adequately on an electric ring.

With a thermostatically-controlled heater it is much easier to keep the wax at a constant temperature. If the wax is overheating and

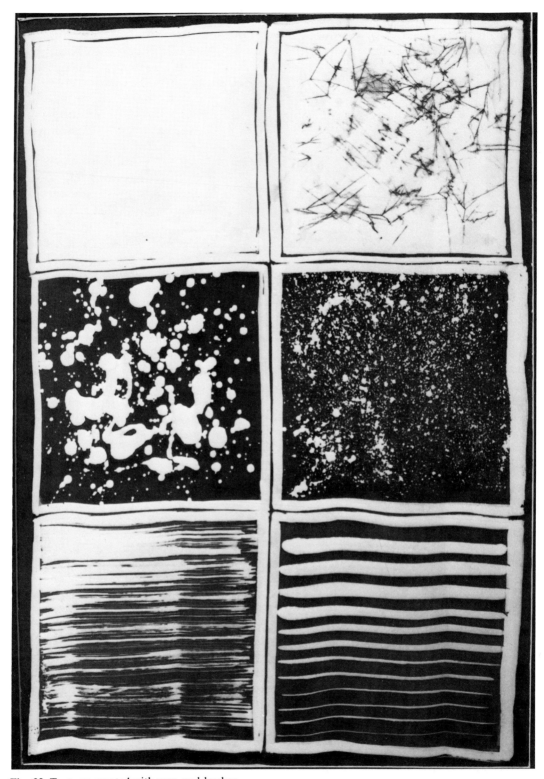

Fig. 32 Textures created with wax and bushes

starts to smoke, turn it off for a while to cool.

As the wax is applied to the silk it should leave a transparent line. If the wax sits on the surface of the silk, remaining hard and white, it has not penetrated the fibres of the fabric and will not protect it from the dye. If the wax has been allowed to overheat, it will run and spread too far, and the brushes will also be quickly ruined.

Equipment for Application of Wax

There are various tools which can be used to apply the molten wax to the stretched fabric.

Brushes
Various brushes can be used. For more information on choice and care of brushes see p. 21. Using a brush to apply the wax is quick and easy, and many textures can be obtained. The lines formed with a brush will vary in width and density.

The samples in Fig. 32 show six different textures that can be created by using different brushes:

1. When a large plain area is required a household or flat-headed brush is ideal. If an area of non-textured colour is required, spread the wax very thickly or apply two coats. The way in which the wax is applied to the silk by the brush can affect the texture created after painting with dye. Random brush-strokes can produce a marbled effect, whereas regimented lines can be achieved by using straight brush-strokes.
2. Once an area has been covered with molten wax and the wax has cooled, the silk can be removed from the frame and crumpled in the hands. Re-stretch the silk on to the frame and paint with dye – this will create a crackled texture.
3. Random drips of wax are produced by shaking a hot wax-filled brush over the silk.
4. A finer spattered effect can be obtained by flicking the tip of a bristle brush against the end of your finger and nail. Alternatively, if this proves too painful, flick the bristle against the side of a ruler or brush handle. Experiment on a test sample as the liquid wax can spatter where it is not wanted. Protect other areas with polythene or thick paper. With practice, it is possible to direct the spray to create the effect of movement. This spattering of the wax can be put to good use for softening a hard edge, snow scenes, blossom and seascapes.
5. A very stiff fan or bristle brush can create a fine linear texture resembling woodgrain. This works well when the wax has been allowed to cool slightly on the bristles. Draw the bristles lightly across the surface of the silk. Interesting textures can be created by combining horizontal and vertical lines, resulting in a checked or woven look.
6. Varying widths of line can be obtained depending on the brush used. However, if a long line is required it is extremely difficult to maintain a continuous line with an even width. The brush has to be reloaded frequently with wax and it is difficult to continue without the joins being obvious. If a thin continuous line is required it is advisable to use a Tjanting.

Tjantings
The Tjanting is a small copper bowl attached to a wooden handle with one or more spouts leading from its base. They are sold with different-sized spouts which produce lines of varying thickness. The tool is dipped into the molten wax to fill the copper reservoir. The liquid wax is then applied to

Fig. 33 Tjantings

the fabric through the spout or spouts.

Hold the Tjanting in your hand as if you are holding a pen. Dip the bowl into the molten wax. Leave for a few seconds to allow the copper bowl to heat. Keep the liquid wax in the reservoir at an even level. Tilt back the spout, or cover the tip with cotton wool, while transferring the Tjanting and wax to the silk. When transferring the wax in the Tjanting keep a cloth, tissue or cotton wool pad underneath to prevent drips ruining the design. Wipe the underside of the bowl frequently to remove dripping wax.

Trail the spout gently across the silk, and you will find that a thin wax line appears. This trail of wax varies according to its temperature. If the wax is the correct temperature a trail of fine, even, transparent lines is formed; if the wax is too hot, it will spread unevenly. The Tjanting spout may block if the wax solidifies in the bowl. If this happens, clear the spout with a fine wire.

Long, flowing lines can be achieved with a Tjanting; conversely, it is also capable of small, intricate designs. Tjanting work takes practice and mistakes are difficult to remove, but these can sometimes be made to form part of the design.

Figs 34 and 35 show a Tjanting exercise of patterns that can be easily created with a single-spout Tjanting. We suggest you try a test sample like this before starting a larger piece of work.

Other Applicators for Wax

Wax can also be applied to the silk with cotton buds, metal printing blocks and Tjaps. A Tjap is a copper printing block mounted on wood. It is commonly found in Indonesia and is used for repeat designs. The Tjap is not dipped into the molten wax but pressed on to a wax-soaked pad before being placed on the silk.

Fig. 34 Use of Tjanting

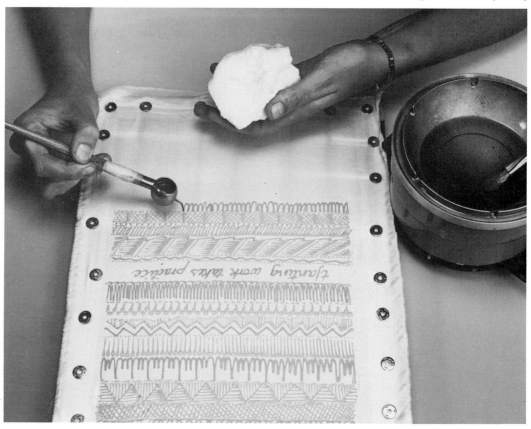

Fig. 35 Dyed Tjanting work

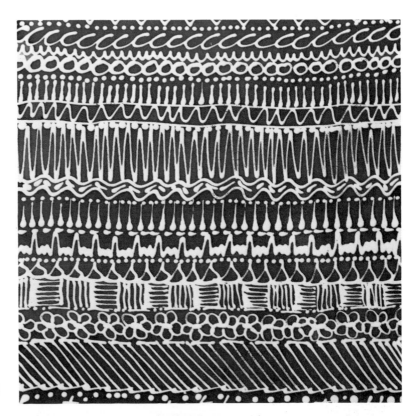

Fig. 36 Use of Tjanting on large parrot sarong

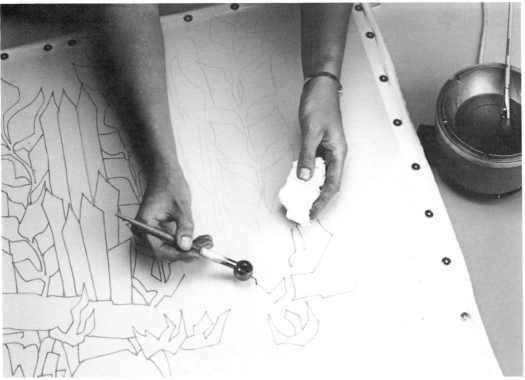

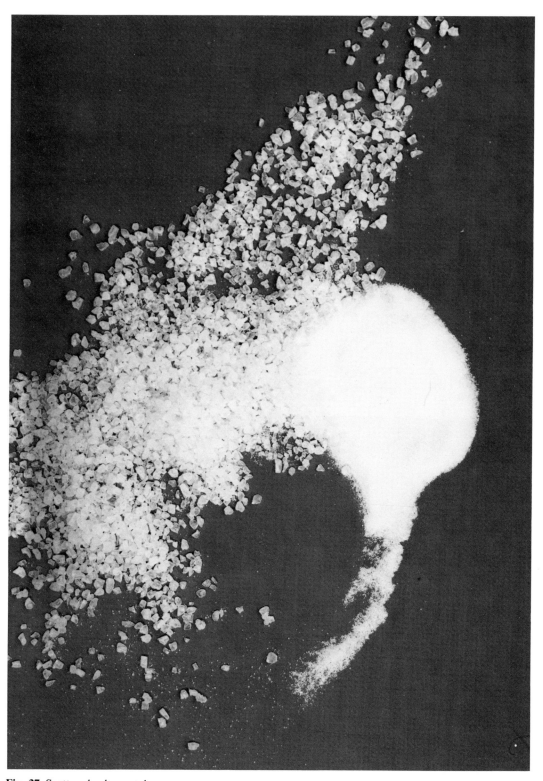

Fig. 37 Scattered salt crystals

6

Salt, sugar & alcohol

Alcohol

There are different strengths of alcohol available; the purer the alcohol, the more effective the result. Try to obtain pure ethyl alcohol which can then be diluted with water, although this is difficult to buy without a permit. Medicinal alcohol, methylated spirits and surgical spirit can be used and are obtainable at chemists and DIY shops. Always keep alcohol away from naked flames.

On the continent it is possible to buy ethyl alcohol over the counter at chemists, but a far cheaper alternative is methanol, which is available at DIY shops.

Interesting effects and textures can be created using salt, sugar and alcohol.

Salt

There are several qualities of salt available. Each will produce a different texture when used in conjunction with the dye. Fine table salt and sea, dishwasher or rock salt are easily available. More difficult to find, as it comes from Switzerland, is the rounder pearl salt. When not in use, keep the salt in an airtight container, as it is important that the grains remain separate.

Sugar

Sugar can also be used to create interesting textures. A white granulated sugar or the more crystallized versions can be used for this purpose.

Fig. 38 Dyes and equipment

7

Dyes & colour

As the craft of silk painting grows in popularity, many silk-painting dyes have been produced. We have placed these into three categories, depending on their method of fixing. Be careful not to use dyes that need different methods of fixing in the same piece of work.

Steam-fixed dyes

These dyes are produced chemically. Unlike paint, they do not build up on the surface of the silk but are absorbed into the fibres of the fabric. The dye penetrates the material so thoroughly that it is impossible to determine on which side of the fabric the colour has been applied.

These dyes are transparent, therefore when one colour is applied over another colour, the second colour will blend with it instead of covering it. The brightness and permanence of colour is excellent and the fabric retains its unique softness and texture. Once fixed, these fabrics are washable and dry-cleanable. They are non-toxic and odourless and available at craft shops under a variety of brandnames: Dupont, Elbesoie, Knaizeff, Savoir-faire, Néobatik, Prince-color, Super-Tinfix, Batiko.

Iron-fixed Dyes

These dyes are thicker and less transparent than the steam-fixed dyes. When applied to the silk, unless the silk is very fine, these dyes will not completely penetrate the fibres. The reverse side of the design is therefore not as clear and bright. It is easy to tell which is the 'right' side. (This may be a disadvantage when making certain items.)

The iron-fixed dyes do not run as easily as the transparent dyes. After fixing a slightly stiff feel is noticed in the fabric, but this is not so noticeable after washing. This characteristic can prove useful with certain techniques, such as painting directly on to the silk. Once fixed, the dyes are washable and dry-cleanable.

The great advantage of these dyes is the easy-fixing method using a hot iron. They are available in most craft shops under the following brand names: Deka, Elbetex, Texticolor, Setacolor.

Special felt-tip pens filled with silk painting dyes can be used to draw on silk. They are useful for detailed work. Ordinary felt-tip pens should not be used. Brand names are: Setaskrib, Staedtler.

Liquid-fixed Dyes

These dyes are water-based and are fixed using a liquid fixer (see p. 47). They are non-toxic and after fixing they are washable and dry-cleanable. They are available at craft shops under the following brand names: Dryad, Orient Express.

Mixing your Dyes

Dyes are available in a wide range of vibrant colours. However the beginner may want to start with a few colours only and in this case we recommend use of the three primary colours plus black.

When dyes are mixed in a palette or pot, pouring from the bottle can be messy and wasteful. It is a good idea to use either a dropper or the end of your brush.

All the dyes can be intermixed and diluted with water and alcohol for pastel shades. For darker tones black can be added in varying proportions. The iron-fixed dyes differ from the others in that there is a white dye which can be mixed with the coloured dyes for pastel shades.

Once the colours to be used have been decided upon, we suggest a test grid be drawn with gutta on stretched silk and used as a sampler for the dyes. You will notice that once the dye has dried the colour is much lighter than before. It will also be more vivid after fixing.

Quantities of Dye

When painting small areas, do not overload your palette and waste the dye – a little dye spreads a long way. Remember that the thicker the fabric, the more the dye is absorbed. For larger background areas over-estimate the quantity of dye to be mixed in your pot, as it is extremely difficult to obtain the same shade when mixing further quantities. Any left-over dye can be stored for future use in an airtight glass container.

When mixing a new colour always start with the lighter colour first; the darker colours should be introduced a little at a time as they are very strong.

Diluting the Dyes

When lighter shades are required, the dye must be diluted, using water, alcohol or diluent, depending on the make. Although we have had success with tap-water, manufacturers sometimes recommend rainwater or distilled water. For smoother application of the dyes over large areas, it is advisable to use diluent or an alcohol/water mix with the dye. It is recommended that at least 10% of water, alcohol or diluent is added to the concentrated dyes. This will not change the shade, will save money and will also avoid an excess of colour after fixing.

The dyes can be diluted from 1 part to 10 parts diluent depending on how deep or pale a shade is required. All the dye brands have different instructions, so read the label. For your own reference, it is a good idea to make a colour chart with notes on how these colours have been mixed or diluted.

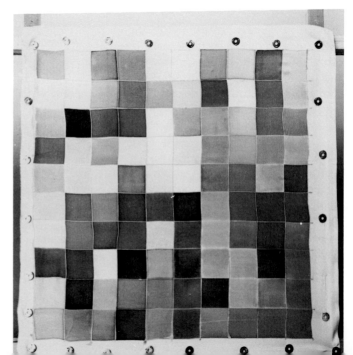

Fig. 39 Test colour chart

Storing your Dyes

All dyes should be stored in airtight containers, away from direct light and in a cool place. Diluted and mixed colours will keep in sealed glass or polythene containers for future use.

Colour

Obviously everyone has favourite colours and you will naturally choose those which suit your taste and style. The following section on colour is included as basic information on how to mix colours and to help you develop your awareness of colour combinations.

Primary Colours

There are three main or primary colours: red, blue and yellow. These are known as primary colours because they are not produced by mixtures of any other colour. These three colours can be mixed in different proportions to produce any colour.

Secondary Colours

The secondary colours are green (a mixture of yellow and blue), orange (a mixture of red and yellow), and purple (a mixture of red and blue).

The primary and secondary colours make up the six major hues in the spectrum.

Tertiary Colours

Tertiary colours are mixtures of primary and secondary colours. They are yellow-green, blue-green, blue-purple, red-purple, red-orange and yellow-orange.

The Colour Wheel

The colour wheel is a chart of the whole spectrum of colours arranged in a circle. Similar colours, next to each other on the colour wheel, are called hues, but hues are distinct one from another. To change the hue of a colour another colour must be added; for example blue added to green results in a greenish-blue. Depending on the amount of each colour mixed, wide varieties of hue can be obtained.

Black and white have no hue. Several hues which are next to each other on the colour wheel can form a related colour scheme. If you lack confidence in your colour planning or are uncertain which colours to choose, you are almost guaranteed an effective result if you choose three or four neighbouring hues. These related colours can give brilliance and depth to each other. See p. 49 for a detailed colour wheel.

Complementary Colours

Complementary colours are sometimes known as contrasting colours. Each colour in the spectrum has its own complementary colour, the opposite one on the colour wheel: red/green, blue/orange, purple/yellow. Complementary colours have their own characteristics: the yellow/purple pair are both the lightest colour and the darkest, the red/green pair are equal in tone, and the orange/blue pair are the warmest and coldest colours in the circle.

When planning your colour scheme, remember that complementary colours placed side by side are strong and vibrant. They can be toned down by separating them with an area of neutral colour such as beige or grey. Should your work need enlivening, a dash of a complementary colour may brighten up the overall effect.

Tints and Tones

Tints and tones refer to the lightness and darkness of a colour. A hue mixed with white gives a tint and a hue mixed with black gives a tone. The illustration on the full-colour page shows a chart of the tints and tones of three colours: strong pink, green and blue. Paler shades are produced by adding water and alcohol to the dyes in varying quantities. See p. 40 on dyes.

A monochromatic colour scheme can be created by using one hue only, by adding varying amounts of black and white (water and alcohol with dyes). When mixed with grey a hue becomes much softer and less intense.

8

Fixing & washing

The dye needs to be fixed permanently into the silk to allow it to be washed and to prevent fading. There are several ways in which this can be done, depending on the dye used. It is very important to check which method of fixing is to be used when purchasing your dyes. Be careful not to use dyes that need different methods of fixing on the same piece of work. The fixing process sets the dye into the silk. Silk which has not been fixed should be kept in a dry, dark place to prevent accidental water marking and fading by sunlight.

The three ways in which dyes can be fixed are by using a steamer, an iron or a liquid fixer.

Steamers

The aniline or transparent dyes require steam for fixing. There are two types of commercially-available steamers, but it is possible to make your own steamer using a pressure cooker. Commercial steamers are expensive and only viable if you are producing a lot of work or they will be used by a group. Some large craft shops run a steaming service; alternatively, enquire at your local drycleaners if they have a steam box.

Pressure Cooker

The pressure cooker is useful for smaller pieces of work. Place each piece of silk flat on top of several layers of paper: either lining,

kraft paper or newsprint. If newsprint is used make sure that the newspapers are at least one month old, otherwise the printing ink may reprint on the silk. To avoid spoiling work in this way it is worth spending a little extra on lining or kraft paper for this purpose. Roll silk and paper together, then flatten and seal the ends using strong adhesive tape. Tuck the ends in towards the centre, then roll and flatten again to form a small, firm package.

Fill the bottom of the pressure cooker with water to a depth of about 2 cm. The water, even when boiling, must never reach the base of the trivet. Place the packages of silk in a basket on the trivet. To prevent the packages being wet by the condensation from the lid, cover them with paper. Finally, a large sheet of foil should cover the whole basket so that the condensation runs down into the water. Seal the lid and cook under pressure for 45 minutes.

After the pressure cooker has cooled, carefully remove the lid, foil and paper. Remove the basket and undo the parcel to reveal your work.

Vertical Steamer

The vertical steamer is a double-walled stainless steel cylinder. The tube rests on a container of water. Many steamers are fitted with an element, but the manual vertical

Fig. 40 Wrapping the silk in fixing paper for the pressure cooker method

steamer uses a gas ring or an electric hot plate. The steamer is sealed at the top by a dome-shaped lid which has a hole in it.

Steamers of this type can accommodate fabric up to 1 m wide, although an extension tube can be fitted for widths up to 150 cm. Depending on the make of steamer, between 30 m and 50 m of fabric can be steamed at one time.

As with the pressure cooker method, the

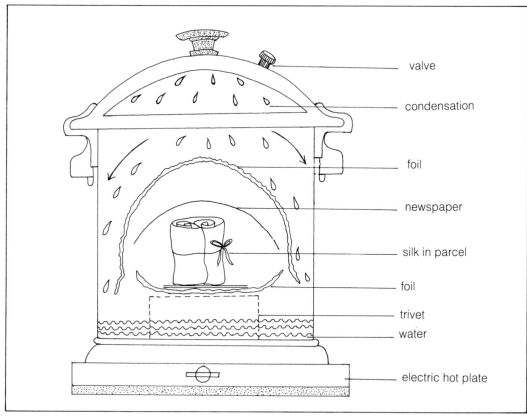

valve

condensation

foil

newspaper

silk in parcel

foil

trivet

water

electric hot plate

Fig. 41 Pressure cooker

Fig. 42 Preparing the fixing

silk must be rolled in paper before steaming. It is important to use the correct paper for rolling the fabric: lining paper or undyed kraft paper is suitable. Roll the paper at one end to form a rigid tube. Carefully lay out pieces of work on the remaining paper, making sure that excess wax and creases have been removed. Individual pieces of work must not touch. Place work in the centre of the paper leaving a margin of approximately 5 cm at each side. If coloured or metallic guttas have been used, paper should be placed on top of the silk as an added protection. It is advisable to do the same where wax, alcohol, sugar, salt or very dark, strong dyes have been used. Slowly and carefully roll the paper up, keeping the edges even. Continue, rolling the paper only, for at least 1 m and seal the edge using strong adhesive tape. Seal each end of the tube with three layers of foil and secure with tape.

Carefully lower the tube down into the cylinder on to the ring at the base, making sure that it does not touch the cylinder walls. Secure the top ring and seal with the dome-shaped lid. Fill the base container with water and then place the cylinder on top. Boil the water and steam for approximately three hours. (Wool will need four hours.) The thicker the fabric, the longer the fixing time will need to be. The cylinder is double-walled so that when the steam rises it condenses under the dome-shaped lid and runs down between the walls to the base for re-use. The dyes are set permanently into the fabric by the steam.

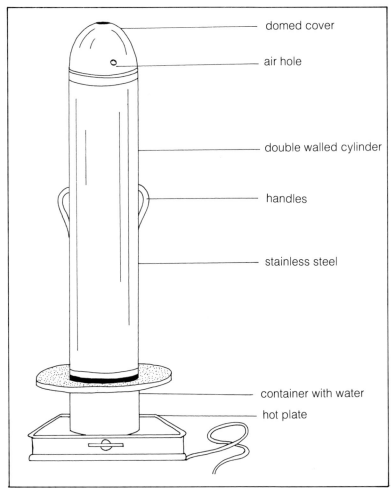

domed cover

air hole

double walled cylinder

handles

stainless steel

container with water

hot plate

Fig. 43 Vertical steamer

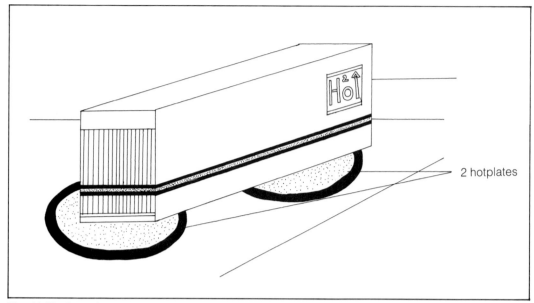

2 hotplates

Fig. 44 Horizontal steamer

The same fixing paper can be used twice providing it has no stains. However if it is re-used the fixing time must be lengthened by one hour because the paper may have lost some of its permeability and absorbency. A prolonged fixing time will not harm the silk, but it may become slightly yellow and the parts near the end of the roll will discolour as the paper cannot absorb all the steam.

Horizontal Steamer

This is a long stainless steel box which can be heated on a gas or electric cooker. It can accommodate approximately 18 m of fabric up to 90 cm in width. Once again, make sure no water penetrates the roll of paper and silk. Use the same method as for the vertical steamer. The water is held in the base of the box and the steaming takes one hour.

The steaming process very slightly alters the colour of the natural silk, so if you are making a garment that includes an undyed piece of silk, remember to fix this at the same time.

Faults, prevention and remedies

a. Watermarks or rings on the silk after it has been removed from the steamer may have been caused in one of the following ways: too much water in the base of the pressure cooker; inadequate protection of the silk with paper and foil; or the silk being placed too near the edges of the paper when rolled.

Once watermarks have been made they are impossible to remove, other than repainting stained areas with a darker dye to cover the fault. Once repainted, it is necessary to fix the work again.

b. Occasionally the kraft paper or newsprint sticks to the gutta lines. This happens when the gutta is too thick. To prevent this, either dilute the gutta using a thinning agent, or use a finer nozzle to apply the gutta.

The paper can be removed by soaking the article in white spirit. Pour white spirit into a screw-top jar, add the silk and shake thoroughly until the gutta dissolves and the paper is detached. This process is not possible if metallic and coloured guttas have been used as the white spirit will remove them. Working with white spirit can be dangerous. Remember to ventilate the room, or work outside. When you have finished, the silk needs to be washed several times in warm soapy water to remove the smell.

46

c. When dark dyes, coloured gutta, alcohol, sugar, salt and wax have been used, reprinting may occur on the roll in the steamer. To prevent this happening, make sure the silk has the added protection of extra paper. If the fault is pronounced, the only remedy is to redesign your work around the fault.

d. Creases may be found in the silk once the paper is removed. To prevent this happening, iron the fabric before rolling in paper. Creasing is more likely to occur when the pressure cooker method is used, as the packages of silk and paper are very tightly rolled.

The creases can be removed by washing the silk in warm water and ironing with a steam iron. This process may need to be repeated.

Fixed by Iron

The dyes which require heat for fixing are the alizarine-based dyes. These dyes are fixed by ironing thoroughly with a hot dry iron on the reverse side of the fabric. They can be washed and dry-cleaned after heat-setting.

Faults that may occur

When ironed, coloured and metallic guttas may print on to your ironing board. If silk is then moved and ironed further there is a danger of the gutta marks reprinting on your work. Make sure kraft or lining paper is used to cover the ironing board and adjusted if printing of gutta has occurred.

Liquid Fixer

Some dyes can be used in conjunction with silk paint liquid fixer to make them light fast, washable and dry-cleanable. Ensure silk-painted fabric is thoroughly dry, then coat or soak the silk in the fixer to cure for approximately one hour. (Some fixers have a longer fixing time than others, depending on the make.) The silk is then rinsed in warm water to remove the fixer and any excess colour.

Fig. 45 Fixing by iron

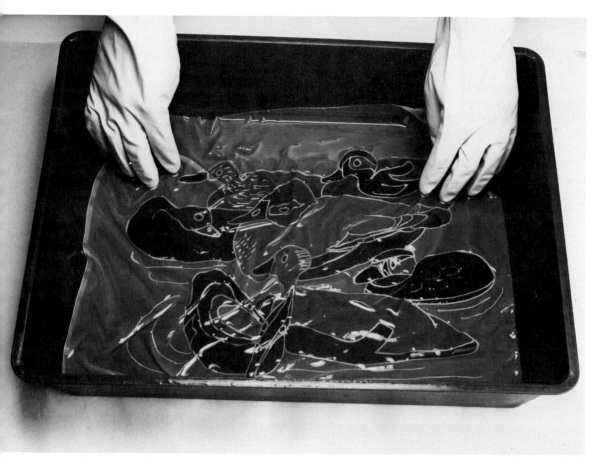

Fig. 46 Liquid fixing

Washing instructions – after fixing

After fixing you will notice that the colours on your work have become more vibrant, and the texture of the silk is softer and has a lustrous sheen. Rinse thoroughly in warm water – this removes any excess dye that may remain in the silk. Large pieces of work need to be spread out to prevent marking, so a large vessel or bath is recommended. If water-soluble gutta has been used, this will be removed at this stage. Gutta can be kept in the fabric but it will give the silk a soft, rubbery texture. If the gutta is removed from the silk a sharp, clear white outline will result. It is possible to remove the gutta by dry-cleaning or by immersing the silk in a screw-top jar of white spirit. Shake thoroughly until all the gutta has dissolved.

The silk must then be rinsed and washed several times in warm soapy water to remove the smell. When working with white spirit, remember to open your windows or work out of doors. Even after commercial dry-cleaning the silk must be washed to remove excess dye.

After washing, lay silk on a clean tea-towel, roll up gently and pat to remove excess moisture. We suggest the silk is ironed straight away while still damp, as the creases will be removed and a fine sheen appears on the surface. Iron the silk with either a steam iron or an ordinary iron on a medium heat-setting. If there is gutta on the silk, iron the fabric on the back to prevent sticking.

Your silk painting is now ready to be sewn or mounted.

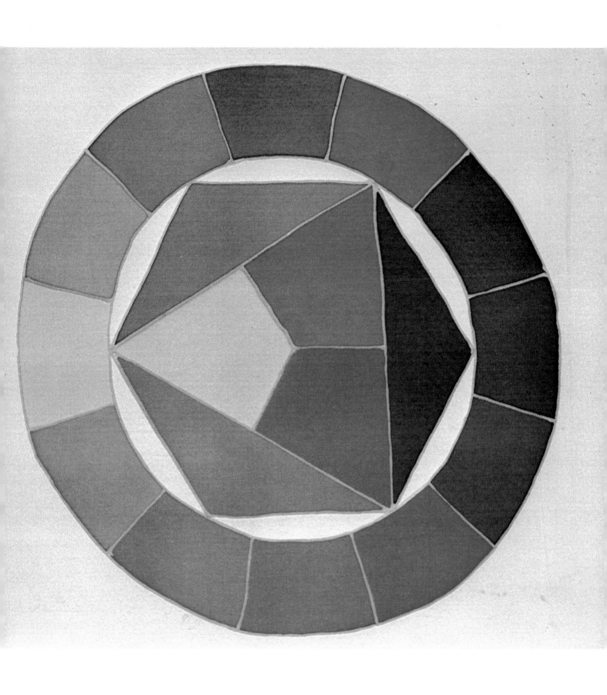

1. Colour wheel

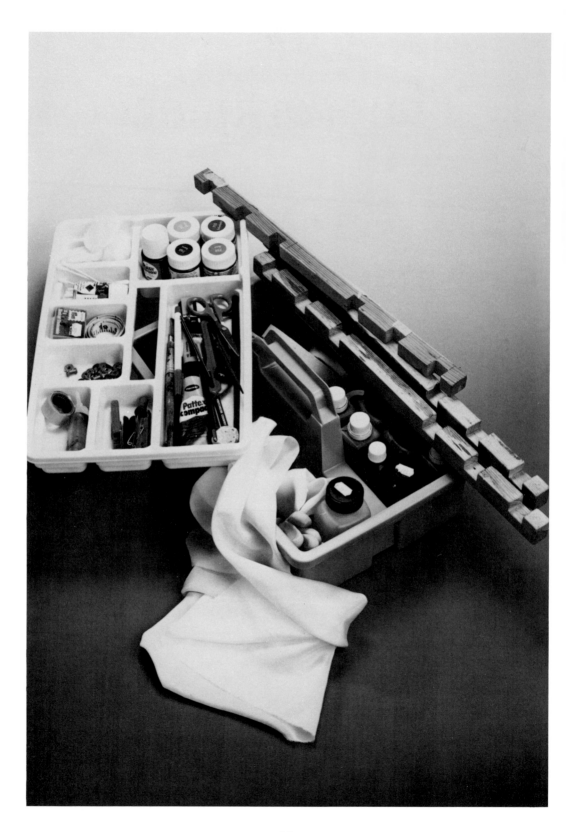

9

The workplace

Painting on silk is an ideal hobby; although a table is needed, all the equipment can be stored away in one small box. The space needed to set up all the equipment need not necessarily be large.

A flat surface is needed to work on because the colours run, and so a table of some sort is necessary. The size of the table depends on the size of frame being used. Sometimes it is easier to stand while painting large pieces; make sure the table is at a good working height to prevent aching shoulders and back. If you have a large enough room, ensure freedom of movement around the table; this helps when working on large frames.

The ideal work-surface is one of white melamine, which can be scrubbed to remove all dye and stains. The painted silk shows its true colours against a white background. However, if a special table cannot be set aside for your painting, and the dining or kitchen table must be used, make sure it is adequately protected with a large sheet of polythene.

The workroom should be light and airy. If the room is too hot, you could find that the dyes are drying too rapidly and unevenly on the silk. It is much easier to paint in daylight, but remember that strong direct sunlight may fade your work if it is left exposed for too long. At night, an extra spotlight may be needed to illuminate your work.

It is not necessary to have a sink in the workroom, but, as with all painting, access to water for diluting dyes and cleaning brushes is needed. If you are working in a carpeted room, beware of spilling dyes; if you are a clumsy worker, protect your carpet.

It is also sensible to protect your clothing, especially sleeves and cuffs, when working with dyes. Roll up your sleeves if possible or wear a thick, long-sleeved overall. When working with cotton wool soaked in dye, we suggest that thin rubber or surgical gloves be worn. It is extremely difficult to remove dye stains from clothing. Dye can be removed from fingers and hands by constant washing with a strong soap and a nail-brush or, if immediate removal of dye is required, use diluted bleach with care.

Fig. 47 Silk painting equipment

2. Related colour scheme

Part two

Techniques

Fig. 48 Sources of design

54

10

The design

The success of your painting can depend upon the design. Any design can be used, but you will soon find that certain designs lend themselves to particular silk painting techniques. Any design used with the serti technique should not be too complicated initially. Large background areas are quite difficult to paint and are therefore best avoided by beginners. As your skill increases, you will be able to attempt more intricate motifs.

Naturalistic designs are ideal for all of the silk painting techniques. As you learn the techniques described in this book you will come to realise which designs suit certain techniques; seascapes and snow scenes are particularly effective when wax is used; a repeat pattern or design can be easily stencilled or sprayed, and landscapes lend themselves to the watercolour technique.

For your design, look around you and take your ideas from what you can see. Make sketches or take photographs, which can be enlarged or reduced in the following way.

Enlarging your Design

Draw a grid of approximately 2.5 cm (1 inch) squares on your original sketch. Decide on the size of your finished work and draw another larger grid. This grid must have exactly the same number of squares as are on the sketch. Working carefully square by square, reproduce the small sketch on the large grid. You will now have enlarged your design to the required size. The same can be done, by reversing the process, to reduce the size.

Transferring your Design

Your design, which is now the required size on paper, must be transferred on to the silk. It is helpful to make the outline bolder on the paper by using a permanent ink pen so that the design shows clearly through the silk.

At this stage you may want to decide on the techniques to use and a colour scheme. Make notes on your drawing.

If you are tracing your design on to the silk, it is best to tape the design and silk to a flat surface to prevent them moving. Masking tape is ideal for this purpose, as it is removed very easily. Lightly trace the motif on to the silk using a fine pencil. Alternatively it is possible to buy a fabric-marking pen for this purpose. The ink from these pens disappears after 72 hours, so use them with caution, remembering to finish your work before the outline vanishes.

The pattern and silk can also be placed on a raised pane of glass with a lamp underneath to allow you to see the design through the silk. The outline can be traced directly on to the silk.

If you are reluctant to attempt your own

Fig. 49 Chosen objects for design

Fig. 50 Sketch being enlarged

Fig. 51 Tracing the design on to the silk

Fig. 52 Iris design stretched on to the frame

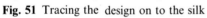

design, prepared transfers can be bought and ironed on to the silk. The outlines will eventually be removed by frequent washing. The designs are often intricate as these are mainly used for embroidery.

Sometimes clear, simple designs can be seen through a fine silk, and it is therefore not necessary to trace the design. The design can be placed under the frame, close enough to be seen but without touching the silk.

The silk is now ready to be stretched onto the frame (see p. 19).

3. Waterlily scarf (serti technique)

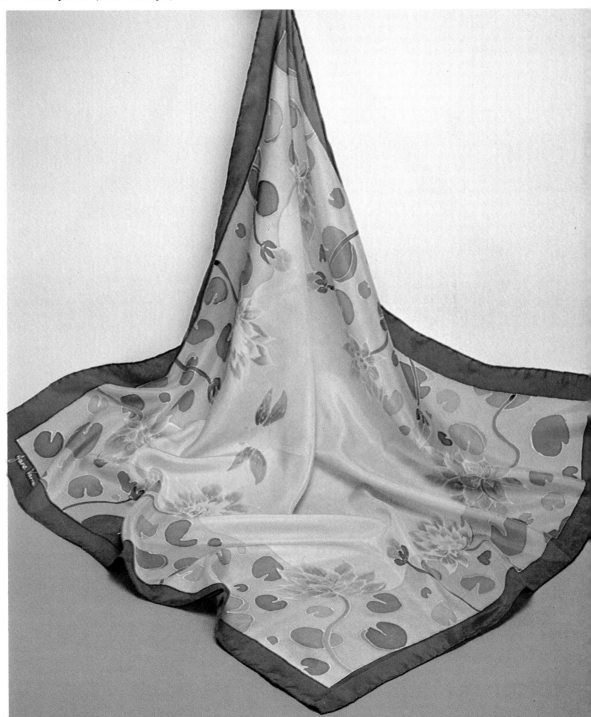

Fig. 53 Silk painted scarf

11

Serti

The Serti technique involves drawing fine lines of gutta on to the silk to outline the design. These lines stop the dyes spreading into each other. The liquid dyes are then painted directly on to the silk and fixed into the fabric.

Equipment needed

Silk
Frame and pins
Masking tape
Dyes and palette
Brushes and applicators
Pipette and nibs or cone
Water, alcohol and diluent

Application of Gutta

First, a decision must be made on the colour of the gutta and which nib and pipette or cone to use. It is very important to check the consistency of the gutta, otherwise the barrier it creates may not be dye-proof. Holding the pipette like a pen, squeeze gently with your fingers to force out the gutta. The gutta process is rather like icing a cake: you must squeeze steadily to produce an even flow. The line formed must be continuous. Always pull the pipette towards you otherwise the tip of the nib may catch in the silk and the line will be jagged. You may hear a slight scratching noise as the nib is pulled over the fibres of the silk; this is nothing to worry about.

Try to hold the pipette at an angle of 45 degrees and exert enough pressure to make the gutta penetrate the silk. To check that the gutta has gone through the silk turn the frame over and you should be able to see a transparent line. If in doubt, apply another line of gutta on to the back of the silk. On thicker fabrics such as wool or wild silk, a thicker nib or just the spout of the pipette can be used. It is useful to hold a tissue in your hand when applying the gutta, as the excess collects around the nib.

Care must be taken not to smudge the gutta line as it remains sticky for some time. It is a good idea to start the outlines at the top and work down keeping your hand and wrist above the surface. Make sure cuffs and loose-fitting sleeves do not smudge your work.

Faults that may occur when applying gutta

1. **The gutta line is too thick and uneven.** This is because the nib-hole or tip of the cone is too large. To remedy this, make a new cone or use a smaller nib.
2. **The silk becomes accidentally smudged or marked with gutta.** These marks may have been caused by the silk touching the work table, the gutta touching the frame or smearing with the forearm. To prevent this, restretch the silk until taut and then insert a pencil between the silk and the

4. Art Nouveau head (coloured gutta, serti technique)

5. Stained glass window (black gutta, nib No. 9, serti technique)

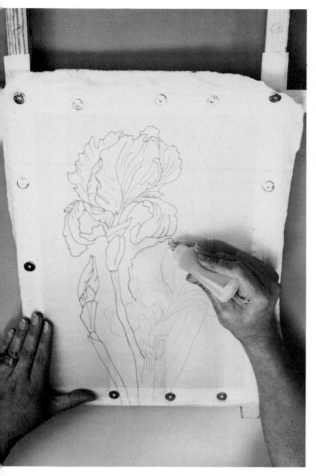

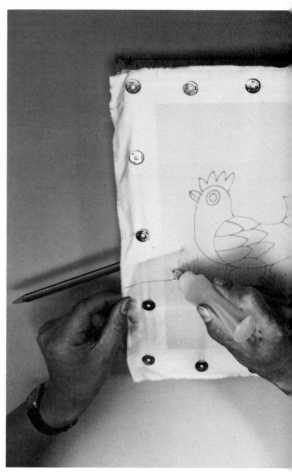

Fig. 54 Application of gutta

Fig. 55 Raising the silk

frame to raise certain sections.

There are two ways of trying to remove unwanted gutta marks:

a. Try to clean the stain by placing a folded tissue under the area and rubbing gently using a cotton bud dipped in the appropriate thinning agent or white spirit. This process may need to be repeated several times until the gutta is removed.

b. Camouflage the mistake by enlarging the design.

3. a. **The gutta is to thick and may remain sticky.** This may be because of age.

However some makes of gutta are thicker than others. The solution to this problem is simple: add a few drops of thinning agent and shake well until the right consistency is obtained. If the gutta remains sticky, it should be removed after applying the dyes or after fixing.

b. **The gutta is too thin.** This is because too much thinning agent has been added. Prevent this by adding some thick undiluted gutta or by allowing the gutta and thinning agent to stand exposed to the air. In time, the thinning agent will evaporate result-

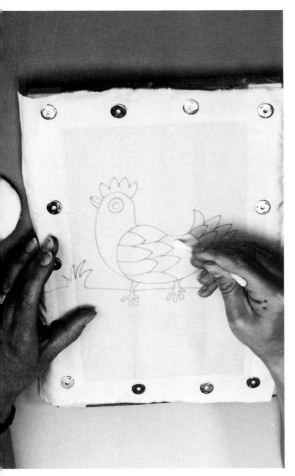

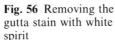

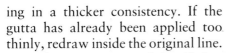

Fig. 56 Removing the gutta stain with white spirit

Fig. 57 Camouflaging the mistake by adding extra feathers

ing in a thicker consistency. If the gutta has already been applied too thinly, redraw inside the original line.

c. **Gutta has not penetrated the silk but remains on the surface.** This will happen if the gutta is too thick (see a) or if a thicker silk or fine wool has been used. On a thicker fabric it may be necessary to gutta on the reverse side to ensure that the gutta has penetrated the fibres.

d. **The gutta has not formed a continuous line.** This may be because of carelessness in the application of the gutta, so that tiny gaps have been left in the gutta line. It may also be because of the pressure exerted on the pipette and the speed at which the line is produced. Ensure that the silk is dry and check that the gutta line is continuous. Carefully re-apply gutta over any gaps. Be careful not to press too hard with the nib on the silk and work slowly to allow a steady flow of the gutta.

e. **The gutta is of a poor quality**. It is always worth buying a good quality gutta as there is no way of improving an unsatisfactory product. The only remedy is to buy a new brand of gutta.

6. Delphiniums (wax technique)

7. Herbaceous border
(wax technique)

8. Foxgloves
(wax technique)

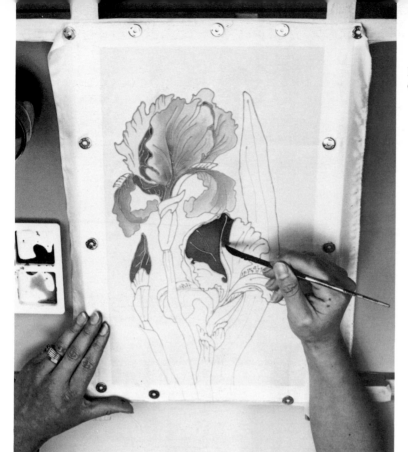

Fig. 58 Painting the iris design

Fig. 59 Painting the background

Fig. 60 Completed iris design

Application of Dyes

Start painting your design with the dyes, working fairly quickly. For preparing and mixing the dyes see pp. 39–40. Light colours should be applied first and the dye should be allowed to flow up to the gutta line. The dye must be worked into the fibres of the silk using the tip of the brush, otherwise uneven colouring may occur. When shading, paint the light colours first then introduce the darker tones carefully. Never overload your brush, as a little dye will go a long way.

When painting large areas, speed is essential, otherwise water lines or rings will appear on the silk. It is best to use foam pads, cotton pads or cotton wool. Fill in enclosed sections first, then work continuously over the silk. For difficult areas, have a finer brush at hand. Never re-touch areas that have already dried, as they will watermark.

Your painted work is now ready for fixing. At this stage make sure your work is protected from water. If left in direct sunlight before fixing the dyes will fade. Take care of your work.

9. Sunset (diluent, antispread, watercolour technique)

10. Anenome scarf (antispread, watercolour technique)

Faults that may occur when applying dyes

Generally there is no problem with the actual dyes; faults that occur at this stage are due to poor painting technique or gutta application.

1. **Dye bleeds through the gutta line where it is not wanted.** This happens because of the way the gutta has been applied (see faults that may occur when applying gutta p. 59). Dyes also flow over the line if either the brush is overloaded with dye or the brush tip has gone over the line.

   If bleeding occurs, quick action is needed to prevent even more dye escaping. Seal the hole where the dye is escaping with gutta. Sometimes hot air from a hair-dryer will stop further spreading.

   There are several ways to remedy the fault.

   a. Try to remove unwanted dye using cotton buds, tissues and alcohol. Place a folded tissue under the stained area and rub gently using a cotton bud dipped in methanol. Be careful not to use too much methanol or the stain will spread. As the dye is extracted from the silk, renew the cotton bud and tissue.

   b. The above process should only be attempted with the lighter shades of dye. When strong, dark dyes have been used, it will be necessary to alter the design. Use some creative flair, and change the design trying to incorporate the mistake as part of the new design.

   c. If the attempt at cleaning has not been successful and on re-painting still looks patchy, working quickly, create a texture using salt or alcohol (see pp. 99, 107).

Fig. 61 Dye being removed with alcohol

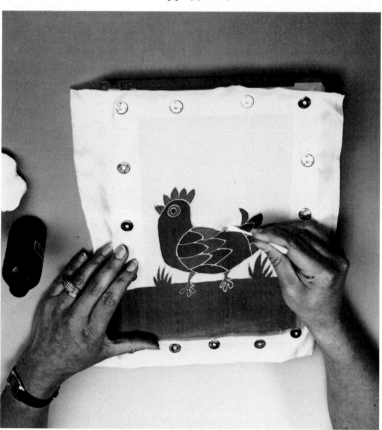

Fig. 62a Mistake is camouflaged by adding extra feathers

Fig. 62b Completed chicken

Fig. 63 Good and bad
painting techniques

2. **Uneven painting of large areas and backgrounds resulting in watermarks and rings.** This occurs when the proportions of dye, water and alcohol are incorrect, or dye has been re-applied to areas that have already dried.

   To prevent this, check the proportions of dye, water and alcohol (see p. 40). If uneven colouring results with pale colours, they can be repainted using a darker, stronger dye. The dye must be worked well into the fabric, over the markings. If the original colour was dark, the only solution is to reprint and add texture using salt or alcohol (see p. 99).

3. **During the course of painting streaks or changes of colour appear.** This is because the brush or applicator has not been thoroughly cleaned.

4. **Marks are caused by silk touching the work-surface.** When painting large background areas the wet fabric stretches and touches the work-surface, marking the silk. Prevent this happening by adjusting the pins to keep the silk taut.

5. **Concentration of dye occurs where the silk touches the frame.** When painting edges or borders the silk should be raised from the frame, otherwise strong lines of dye will appear.

Fig. 64 Lace at the window (tjanting, false batik)

Fig. 65 Daisies showing use of wax and cracking

12

Wax techniques

The most widely-known technique using molten wax and dyes is batik. This ancient craft, dating from the eighth and ninth centuries, is extremely time-consuming. It involves waxing the fabric in (often very intricate) patterns and then immersing the cloth in a dyebath. This process is often repeated several times, each colour being dyed over the previous one to produce a rich harmony.

A less time-consuming approach to this craft is to use silk-painting dyes and wax directly on the stretched silk. This is known as false batik (*faux batik*). There are various other possibilities involving the use of wax combined with silk painting, and it is fun to experiment with all the textures and methods of applying liquid wax.

Equipment needed

Silk
Frame and pins
Masking tape
Dyes and palette
Brushes and applicators
Water, alcohol and diluent
Wax
Heater for wax
Tjanting and wax brushes
Iron and ironing-board
Paper

Rubber gloves
Cotton wool

For the following wax techniques it is necessary to stretch the silk on a frame so that the wax will penetrate through the fibres of the silk. Prepare your design and decide upon the proportions of wax and colours of dye to be used. We suggest you refer back to p. 31 to revise the methods of preparing and applying the wax.

False batik

The end result of a false batik (*faux batik*) can be very similar to that of a true batik. The main saving with this method is in time and dyes used. The silk can remain stretched on the frame throughout this process until the final stage if a crackled texture is desired.

The Butterfly

1. Draw your design on to the silk and stretch it on to the frame. Heat the wax, keeping the wax pot at a temperature of 120°C. Try to keep the hot wax as near to your work as possible; the wax will solidify quickly if it has to be moved very far. When using a brush for the wax keep a cotton pad handy to prevent drips spoiling your work. The colour under every drip of wax will be preserved.

The first stage is to wax all the areas that you want to remain white. For the butterfly the background has been covered with wax, using a flat-headed and a finer sable brush.

Fig. 66 Waxed areas to remain white

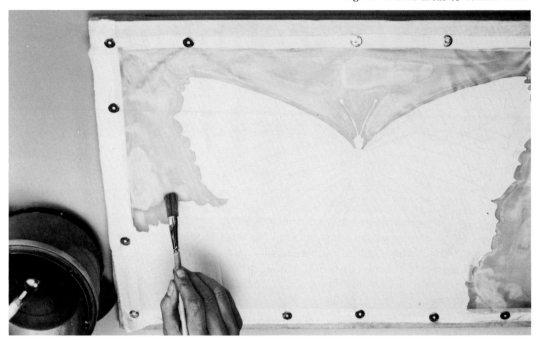

2. With the false batik technique the dye is painted directly on to the silk instead of it being applied in a dye-bath. A large brush or cotton pad can be used in conjunction with the silk-painting dyes. Starting at the top, the dye is applied quickly and evenly over the surface. Allow it to dry. The drying process can be speeded up with the use of a hair-dryer, but care must be taken not to melt the wax.

Fig. 67 Paint with yellow dye

3. When the colour is dry, cover the areas that are to remain yellow with wax. A very fine brush can be used on intricate areas.

Fig. 68 Waxed areas to remain yellow

4. Using a cotton pad and silk-painting dyes, paint the butterfly orange. Allow it to dry.

Fig. 69 Painted with orange dye

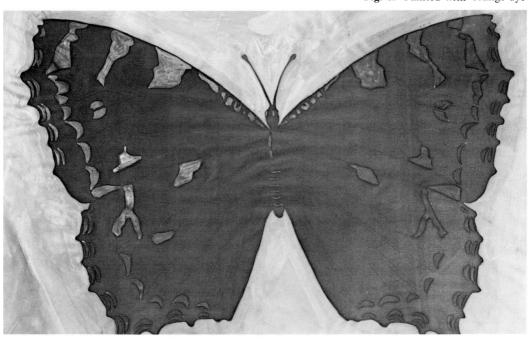

5. Apply the wax to areas that are to remain orange.

Fig. 70 Waxed areas to remain orange

6. Remove the silk from the frame. The characteristic crackle of batik can be obtained by crushing the waxed silk in the hands before the last dye colour is applied.

Fig. 71 Crack silk

7. Restretch the silk on the frame and apply the final dark brown dye. You will notice that the brown dye has penetrated the cracks in the wax that were made by crushing the silk. Allow to dry.

Fig. 72 Painted with brown dye

8. When dry, take the silk off the frame and remove the wax.

Fig. 73 Ironing out wax

Removal of Wax

Most of the wax can be removed from the silk by ironing it between layers of absorbent paper. Do not use newspapers next to your silk as the newsprint will reprint on to your design: use brown, kraft or lining paper. As the wax melts under the heat of the iron it will be absorbed by the paper. Keep replacing the saturated paper with clean layers until as much as possible has been removed. Remember to protect your ironing board with an old sheet and layers of paper. It is extremely difficult to remove all of the wax in this way, but the remaining wax will be removed during fixing. Sometimes a faint grease line is still visible, and to remove this soak the silk in white spirit, see p. 46.

9. The finished work is now ready to be mounted and framed.

When choosing the colours for your project you must plan in advance so as to be able to apply them in the right order. It is necessary to start with the lightest colour first and progress to the darker colours. It is a good idea to make a sample strip to test your dyes as you paint, because when the dyes are painted on top of each other they can mix to create a new colour. For example, when green is painted over red a brownish colour is obtained, not the green you had perhaps imagined; when blue is painted over yellow, green is obtained.

The joy of false batik is that you may use all the colours of your palette, if so desired, on one project. The rule of painting the light colours first still applies, however.

Fig. 74 Finished butterfly

Fig. 75 Herbaceous border

The Herbaceous Border

In the Herbaceous border picture the sky was painted pale blue and covered with wax when dry. The flower heads were all painted different colours, dried and then covered with wax. Some deeper tones were added, and again these were covered with wax. Next, using a cotton pad soaked in pale green dye, the whole picture was evenly covered. This was allowed to dry and the stems and leaves picked out in wax with a fine brush. The final stage before ironing out the wax was a coat of dark green dye, applied with a cotton pad. The spots that remain on the wax after coating with dye create an interesting texture. However if they are not required, these can be removed with a cotton bud while the dye is still wet. Remove all the wax by ironing and soaking in white spirit.

Cracking Methods

The characteristic texture created by cracking the wax can enhance your batik. Depending on the design, you may need to either isolate areas for cracking or crack the whole piece.

To produce the cracking, crumple the work in your hands and then restretch it on the frame. Rub the surface with dye using a cotton pad; the dye will penetrate the cracks. The wax must be dry and hard before crumpling. If it is still malleable, it will not crack.

The delicate veining which results gives the impression of marble. It is difficult to determine the end result and care must be taken not to overcrackle. On pale and intricate work the dye may penetrate too thoroughly and ruin the design. However,

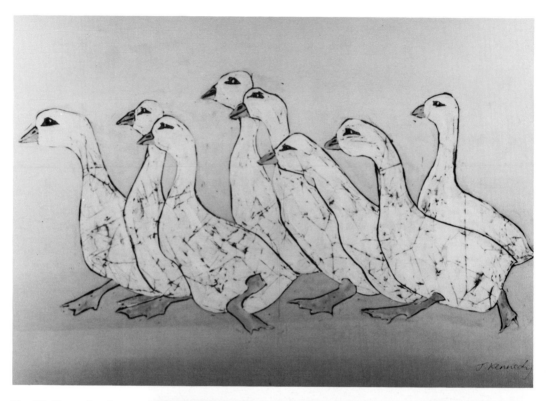

Fig. 76 Geese showing
cracking on bodies only

Fig. 77 Cracking
radiating from centre

Fig. 78 Cracking obtained by pleating and folding

large bright backgrounds can be subdued with cracking. For the right quantities of beeswax to paraffin wax needed to obtain good cracking, see p. 31.

Controlled Cracking

It is possible to control the cracking to a certain extent. The geese shown in Fig. 76 have cracking on their bodies only. This was done by waxing the geese first and cracking those areas. The silk was then restretched and the background painted. The design was allowed to dry, then the background waxed. The whole design was coated with navy-blue dye on a cotton pad covering the whole surface. By this method the cracking appears only on the geese.

In Figs 77 and 78 controlled cracking has been produced by pleating and folding the silk in specific directions.

It is possible to achieve several colour crackings by coating each set of cracks with wax and re-cracking and re-drying.

Fig. 79 Brighton Pavilion showing
continuous Tjanting lines

Tjanting Methods

The Tjanting and how to use it is described
on p. 33. The design of the Brighton Pavilion
is a good illustration of the continuous
flowing lines that can be obtained using a
single-spout Tjanting. Unless you are an
expert, bear in mind, when deciding to use a
Tjanting, that the design may have to be
altered to cover misplaced drops of wax.

The depth of colour in the Brighton
Pavilion picture has been obtained by three
separate coats of wax and dyes.

The Tjanting can also be of use in producing spots and dashes of wax. This method
has been put to good use in the lace curtain
picture.

Other uses of Wax

Wax can also be used in conjunction with
other techniques. When painting on silk
clean white areas can be retained with the use
of wax, and it makes seascapes and snow
scenes particularly effective.

The waves and sea spray in Fig. 81 have
been created with the use of wax. The brush
strokes from the waves, with the spray being
spattered on to the crest of the wave to give
movement, are created using the technique
described on p. 33.

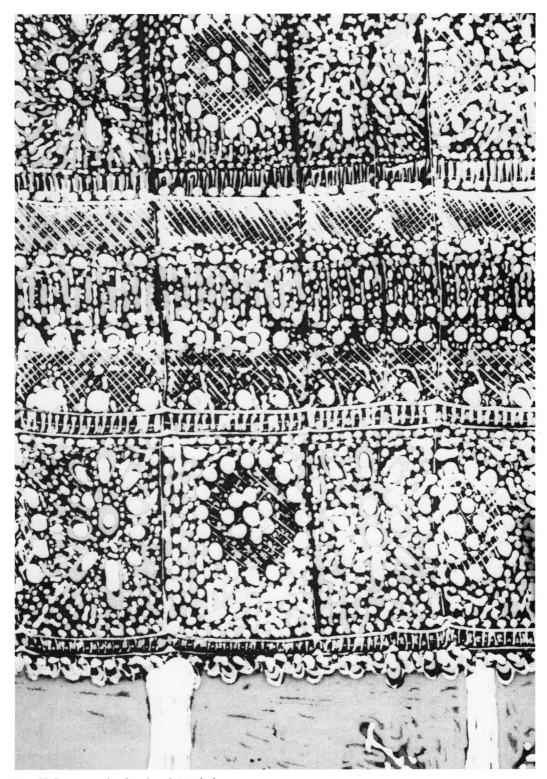

Fig. 80 Lace curtain showing dot technique

Fig. 81 Stormy seascape
showing spattering technique

Faults that may occur and how to prevent them

1. **The dye penetrates the silk under the wax.** This is because the wax is not hot enough on application and remains on the surface of the silk. Once the dye has been applied there is no remedy, but careful checking of the wax at each stage could prevent this. If the wax starts to peel or has not penetrated through the silk, work can be rewaxed on both sides.

2. **After several dyes and crackings the wax tends to disintegrate and flake off.** This can be remedied by recoating with wax to penetrate the silk.

3. **The wax has spread too far over the surface of the silk where it was not required.** This happens because the wax is too hot and has become too fluid. To prevent this use a test sample to try out the flow of the wax. Should this occur the design must be modified to incorporate the mistake. The only way to remove the wax would be to soak in white spirit or dry-clean the fabric, which means the whole project would need to be rewaxed.

4. **Discoloration of wax.** This occurs if the wax has not been allowed to harden and cool before the application of dye. After the removal of wax some unwanted staining may have occurred. Make sure the wax on the silk is cool and hard before dying.

5. **Blobs or drips of wax have fallen in the wrong place.** This is mainly caused by inexpert use of the Tjanting or brush. Do not overload your brush or Tjanting with wax and always keep a tissue or cotton pad handy to catch the drips. It is impossible to remove these blobs, so try to modify your design so as to include them.

6. Any faults that have occurred when applying the dyes have been fully discussed on p. 70.

13
Watercolour

This style enables a freer approach as the dyes are unrestrained by the barriers created by gutta and wax in the serti and wax methods.

Fig. 82 Watercolour seascape

Equipment needed

Silk
Frame and pins
Masking tape
Dyes and palette
Brushes and applicators
Diluent
Water
Antifusant
Epaississant

Painting directly on to the Silk

Various effects can be obtained by painting the dyes directly on to the silk. The dye will run when there is no barrier of gutta or wax to stop it.

The finer silk, such as pongée 5, is used with the transparent dyes. The dye spreads quickly over the fabric as shown in Fig. 83. An entirely different effect can be created by using a thicker silk, for example pongée 10 or crêpe de chine with the iron-fix dyes; you will notice in Fig. 84 that the dye retains a softer outline but does not spread. In this sample the hydrangea was drawn with a disappearing marker pen. A further effect is created by the pen lines which resist the dye before they disappear.

Fig. 83 Hydrangea painted directly on to silk (pongée 5)

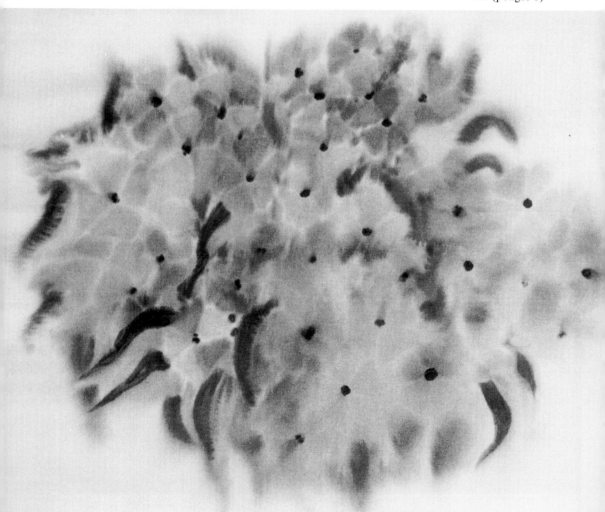

Fig. 84 Hydrangea painted directly on to silk (pongée 10, iron-on dyes)

Backgrounds

Graded wash effects can be produced by blending different colours or tones of one colour into each other. Backgrounds can be extremely difficult to paint evenly. For those who find this hard, large areas can be divided into smaller sections by careful planning when designing. If a very pale background colour is required, it is sometimes easier to paint over the entire fabric, including the design, rather than to paint around an intricate motif. The pale dye on the design would be covered by brighter or darker overpainting. For dilution of the dyes with water and alcohol see p. 40.

The dye should be applied to larger areas using a large brush or cotton pad. Make sure enough dye has been prepared to cover the whole area. Work the dye across the silk quickly and evenly from side to side, working down the fabric. When the brush needs refilling with dye always rejoin at an edge, never in the middle, to avoid a build-up of dye in any one place.

For very large areas wet the whole background with clear water first. The damp surface helps the dye to spread, avoiding hard edges. The silk should be very tightly stretched on the frame, as when it is wet it will stretch slightly and sag.

Fig. 85 Graded wash

Shading

When shading it is necessary to work quickly before the dyes have time to dry. It is important that all your equipment is organised before you start, as speed is essential when using this technique. On very large areas it is often helpful to work with another person.

Start by wetting the entire background with clear water. There are spreading agents available called Diluent, Anti-cerne or Diffusant Fondnet which can be used with water to help the dye spread. These are discussed under the heading *Diluent* (p. 93).

Starting with the darkest dye, evenly coat the fabric, introducing the paler dyes, ending with white, as you move upwards.

To prevent lines forming where you have

Fig. 86 Landscape
created by line building

introduced a new shade, ensure that areas of dye overlap. Rub firmly so that the shades merge into each other. If definite lines have appeared and cannot be rubbed away, they cannot be removed. Do not attempt to repaint, as this will cause watermarks to appear.

If, on the other hand, you wish to use lines, for instance to suggest interesting landscapes or rock formations, they can be created by allowing the silk to dry between each application of dye.

Start by covering the entire background with the palest dye. Leave to dry, then add a deeper tone. Repeat this process several times. Leave the silk to dry naturally. Do not use a hair-dryer, as the dye will need time to spread and reform into the dark dyes.

Fig. 87 Line building using diluent

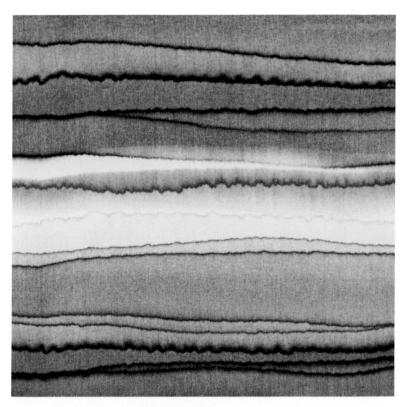

Fig. 88 Spots formed using diluent

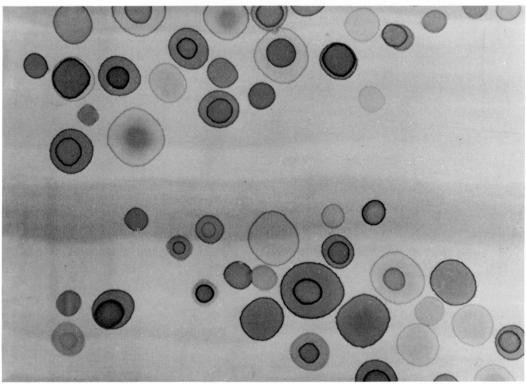

Diluent

Diluent is also known as Anticerne or Diffusant Fondnet. This can be used in place of water to dilute the dyes. The dyes must be diluted by at least 10%; more diluent can be added for pastel colours. Diluent is bought in a concentrated form. Make sure you read the label for specific instructions on how to prepare it for use. Some silk painters use diluent, in preference to water, with all their dyes as it helps even colouration. We suggest it be used instead of water when painting large background areas. Wet the silk with diluent instead of water and then paint or shade with dye. The diluent aids uniform spreading and merging of the dye, avoiding lines and watermarks.

Interesting textures can also be created using diluent and dyes, allowing the silk to dry in between each application.

In Fig. 88 the silk was coated in diluent, then allowed to dry, Diluent was added to coloured dyes and applied using a cotton bud. Darker-edged circles are formed in this way, creating a delicate, interesting effect.

Antifusant

Antifusant is also known as anti-spread. It is a starch-like fluid used to prevent dyes from penetrating and spreading through the fabric. This enables direct painting on to the silk without the colours penetrating. This product is available ready-prepared, but it is possible to prepare your own anti-spread by

Fig. 89 Baby's christening picture painted on anti-spread background

Fig. 90 Vase of tulips painted on anti-spread background

94

mixing Essence F and gutta together. We suggest one part gutta to six parts Essence F. Pour the Essence F and gutta into an airtight container and shake thoroughly. The higher the proportion of gutta, the more resistant the silk becomes to the dye.

Coat the required area with anti-spread using a cotton pad or cotton bud. If a brush is used it must be cleaned in white spirit or Essence F to remove the gutta. The silk must be dried before painting; the drying time can be shortened by the use of a hair-dryer. When it is dry you can paint directly on to the fabric.

Alternatively, anti-spread can be mixed 50/50 with the dyes which can then be used to paint directly on to the silk without having prepared the whole background.

This technique is not entirely suitable for scarves as the dyes do not penetrate the silk, which leaves the underside much paler than the right side. Even after fixing, a stiffness in the silk remains, but this can be removed by frequent washing or soaking in white spirit.

In Fig. 91 the rainbow-shaded spot picture, previously shown in Fig. 88, has had its surface treated with anti-spread and dried. The Japanese-like branches were blown across the silk using dye and a straw. It can be clearly seen how the dye has travelled over the surface of the silk rather than penetrating the fibres and spreading.

Epaississant

Epaississant is also known as dye-thickener. It is a colourless glue-like substance. It is possible to add this thickener to the dyes, thus making it possible to paint direct on to the silk without spreading. Pour a small amount of thickener on to your palette and mix with the dye as required. This thickened dye is very useful for fine detailed work, for example branches, grasses or faces. If large areas are covered with this thickener the texture made by the brushstroke may remain, and the result may be uneven colouration.

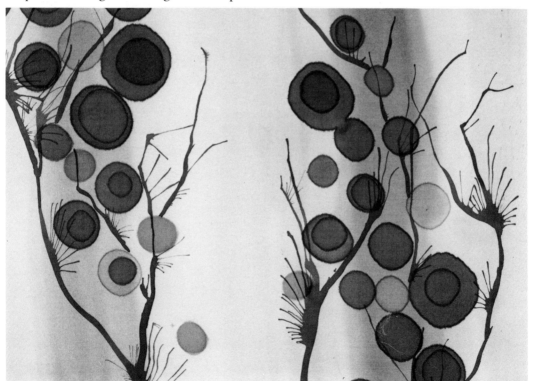

Fig. 91 Blowing technique on anti-spread background

Fig. 92 Landscape using
epaississant on fir trees

11. Art Deco Lady (serti, alcohol technique)

14
Salt, sugar & alcohol

Fig. 93 Flower salt pattern

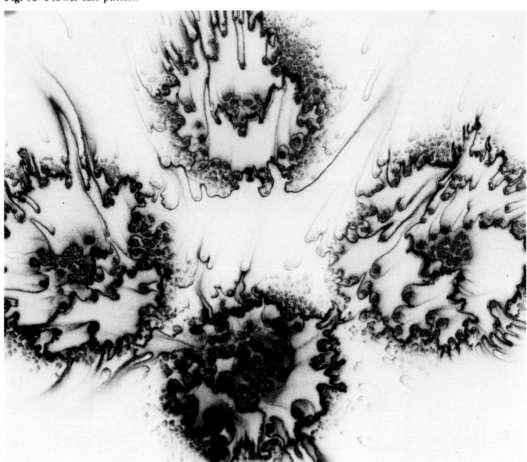

These techniques are very easy. Many spontaneous and interesting effects can be obtained with the use of salt, sugar and alcohol. The varied textures that these create can enliven plain areas of your work.

Equipment needed
Silk
Frame and pins
Masking tape
Dyes and palette
Brushes and applicators
Water
Salt
Sugar
Alcohol
Rubber gloves

Salt
This technique is very simple and produces exciting results. It can be put to good use disguising faults made in the application of gutta and dyes. All that is required is a painted damp background and salt. Sprinkle the salt over the damp background and wait patiently for the results. It may take up to twenty minutes for the silk to dry while the design is forming. You will be able to watch

the colour flow as the salt crystals take up the dye and leave the colour pigments as dark lines and spots. This salt technique requires the use of water rather than alcohol, which evaporates too quickly and so dries the silk.

It is fun to experiment with this technique because quite different results can be obtained by varying the method slightly. Heating the salt before use can produce a stronger reaction.

Different sizes of salt crystals
Rock salt will produce larger forms reminiscent of mountains, forests, caves and craggy rock faces; whereas finer table salt will form feathery effects and naturalistic designs. Pearl salt grains, being uniform in size, produce a more even, rounded design.

Pure, mixed, diluted or different makes of dye
Undiluted pure dyes produce strong dramatic lines and shapes. These shapes are formed where the pigment is drawn towards the silk. A softer, more flowing effect can be created by diluting the dyes with water. Sometimes certain mixed dyes separate slightly while drying, forming shades and

Fig. 94 Effect of salt
crystals after two minutes

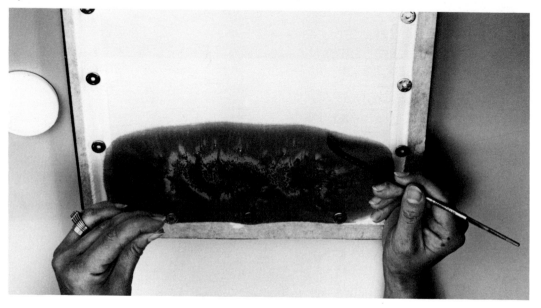

12. Sweet peas (sugar technique)

13. Orchid scarf (serti, watercolour technique)

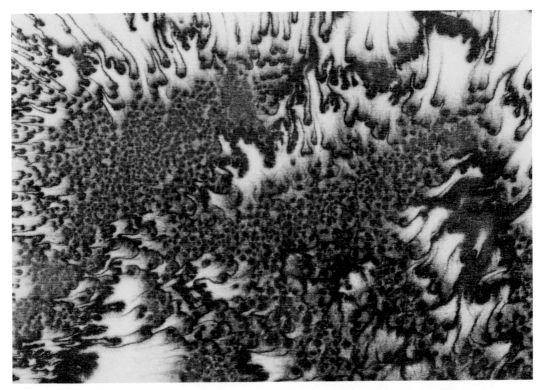

Fig. 95 Use of table salt

Fig. 96 Use of rock salt

tones of their base colours. You will notice a difference in the movement of the pigment between the more liquid transparent dyes and the thicker dyes which need to be heat fixed.

Different grades and textures of silk

The salt reacts with the dye on a smooth fine silk, such as Pongée 5, very effectively, but interesting results can be obtained on the thicker or textured silks. It is wise to experiment on a sample test piece first before embarking on a large project.

Moisture content of the background

It is important that your silk is damp, neither too dry nor too wet. If the background is too dry only round shapes and spots will develop. Conversely, if it is saturated with dye the salt becomes overloaded with the pigment and cannot work effectively.

When working on large areas of silk we suggest you wet the background with water using a large washbrush or cotton wool before applying the dye; this will lengthen the drying time. Make sure your workroom is not too hot when using this technique otherwise the silk will dry too rapidly.

Random and controlled placing of salt crystals

Random

Scattering the salt at random is effective on backgrounds. Apply the salt as you paint, working quickly and steadily before the dye dries. Be careful not to use too much salt, as this hinders the movement. A mottled effect can be created by using several colours intermingled; the salt will blend them together. This is a very quick and successful way to produce a scarf (see Fig. 98).

Fig. 97 Salted flower using iron-on dyes

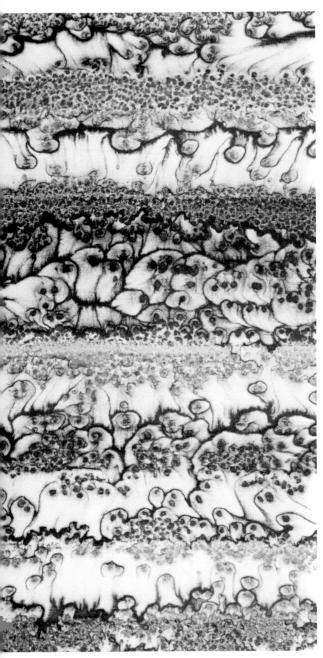

Fig. 98 Use of rock salt
on stripes

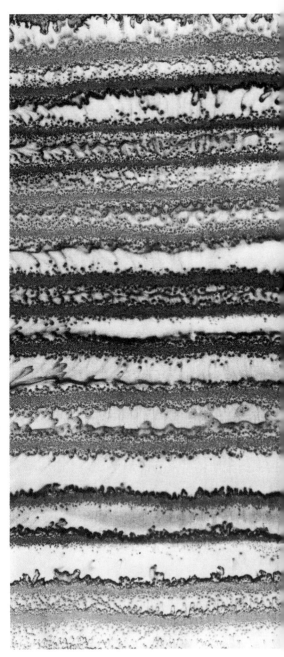

Fig. 99 Use of table salt
on stripes

14. Clematis (spraying)

Controlled

Specific patterns can also be created with this technique. One simple idea is to paint bands of colour in stripes using a thick brush, placing either rock or table salt along the lines where the two colours meet.

Individual circles or flowers can be produced by painting the background one colour, placing a circle of salt on this background (which can be either wet or dry), then adding a few drops of dye to the middle of the circle. This will intensify the flower centre (see Fig. 98). Never paint more than four or five flower shapes at once, because the salt grains only work on wet or damp dye. The circles or flowers should not be too close together or they will run into each other.

If you are using several techniques on one piece of work, always ensure that the salt technique is the last one if possible, as the salt could accidentally fall on an area where it was not wanted. It is most important that no grain of salt find its way via the brush into the dye bottle; it only takes a few grains to ruin the dye.

Always work on a flat, even surface making sure the salt crystals do not move once applied. Leave the work in position until it is completely dry, as any movement may disturb the salt and spoil the design that is forming.

The salt crystals should not be removed until the work is thoroughly dried. Rock salt can easily be brushed from the surface, but finer table salt may stick. If this happens, either scratch off the grains with your nails or remove the work from the frame and gently rub the silk together. The silk should be entirely free from salt before being fixed.

Salt solutions

Another texture can be obtained by using the salt in solution to prevent the dyes from spreading. Make this up with one litre of warm water to 250 grams of salt. Stir and leave to dissolve for one hour. Filter the solution through a filter paper to remove any remaining grains of salt.

Either stretch the silk on a frame and paint the solution evenly on the silk using a sponge applicator or a wide brush, or soak the silk in a bath of salt solution and hang it up to dry. The dye can now be painted directly on to the silk without spreading. The salt particles give an interesting texture to the work.

Sugar

This is not quite as exciting as the salt technique, as it has its limitations. When dampened with dye, the crystals draw dye to a certain extent, but with only a small effect on the texture.

The crystals can be used for an interesting experiment in producing a crusty texture but this will take time. The dye is painted on to thickly-spread groups of crystals and allowed to soak into the sugar for a considerable time without drying out. A damp, cool place should therefore be used to leave the frame and silk. It may take up to four days for the 'experiment' to work. This may be interesting to try as a small project.

Sugar solution

As with salt, the sugar can be mixed with one litre of water to 250 grams of granulated sugar. A solution will form immediately as the sugar dissolves. It is not necessary to filter this.

Stretch the silk on a frame and using a cotton wool pad or sponge applicator paint the silk evenly. When dry, the surface will be less permeable to water and dye. The sugar acts as a resist so that when the dyes are painted on they do not immediately spread. A soft, interesting effect can be shown, rather like that described in the chapter on Watercolour and Antifusant (see p. 87; Sweet peas, colour plate 12).

Alcohol

This technique is also fairly simple and involves the use of dyes and alcohol. For the types of alcohol used see p. 37. The stronger the alcohol and dyes, the more effective the results. Paint the pattern or design on the silk while it is stretched on a frame. It is advisable to try a test sample first before embarking on a large project.

If you are using different colours, make sure they dry first. Always leave a space between the colours, otherwise they will run. It is essential to wait until the work is completely dry. Dip a brush into alcohol and wipe off the excess liquid. Take care not to overload the brush. Alternatively a cotton wool bud dipped in alcohol can produce even, round designs.

The effect created by this technique is opposite to the salt technique as the alcohol disperses the pigment, whereas the salt attracts it. When alcohol is applied to a painted shape or line the centre becomes clear and the pigment layers itself to the edges, thus appearing darker. If this process is repeated several times the centre becomes paler and the outside line becomes more defined. Rub gently with the brush or cotton bud to remove the dye. If further removal is necessary, wash the brush in water but ensure that it is dry before continuing or, if using cotton buds, renew them each time.

Let the silk dry between each application of alcohol. The more pigment in the dye, the stronger the reaction to the alcohol will be. While experimenting with this technique you will notice that certain dyes react more effectively than others. Take care when using alcohol, as it is inflammable.

The alcohol technique is often used in conjunction with the serti and watercolour techniques to give added texture to flat, plain areas. Mistakes can be cleverly concealed, often by applying dabs of alcohol to create texture. Backgrounds which have been unevenly covered with dye can also be camouflaged well.

Fig. 100 Background impregnated with salt solution

15. Roses scarf (thickener)

16. Wisteria picture (spraying)

Fig. 101 Background impregnated with sugar solution

Fig. 102 Effect of alcohol on dye

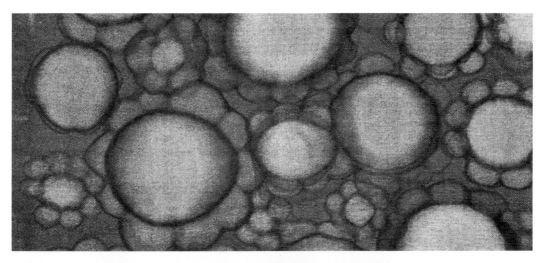

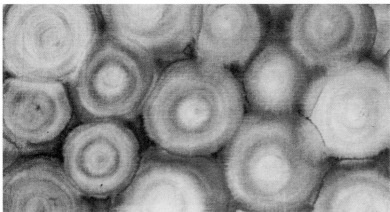

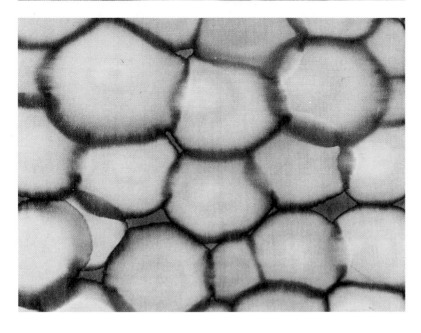

Fig. 103   Fig. 104
Fig. 105 Textures
created using alcohol

17. Parrot sarong (crêpe de chine)

18. Peacock blouse (crêpe de chine)

Fig. 106 Sprayed wisteria

15

Spraying
& stencilling

Stencilling can be used when applying the dye to silk. If your drawing skills are limited, using this technique even simple designs can look very professional, especially when repeated. Stencilling is now regaining popularity and ready-made stencils are available in decorating shops.

Equipment needed

Silk
Frame and pins
Masking tape
Dyes and palette
Brushes
Air spray or diffuser
Water, diluent and alcohol
Stencil paper
Cutting tool
Tracing paper
Metal ruler
Cutting board
Antispread (antifusant)
Thickener (epaississant)

Stencil Paper

To make the stencil it is best to use stencil paper, which is specially treated to withstand repeated applications of dye. Alternatively, thick acetate film, heavy paper or card may be used. If a repeat pattern is required, stencil paper must be used (this can be bought from art supply shops).

Cutting Tools

A sharp cutting tool is needed to cut the stencil. Depending on the thickness of the paper you will need either a light craft knife or a heavy-duty stanley knife. These are available from craft shops and have removeable blades.

It is important to have a sharp pointed blade for cutting your stencil. A good cutting tool which has a multi-edged blade is available. The tip of this can be snapped off when it has become blunt.

A metal ruler is also useful for cutting straight lines, as a wooden ruler chips easily. It is necessary to cut on a wooden board – if you are intending to do a lot of stencilling it may be worth investing in a special cutting mat. These mats are excellent as cutting does not mark the surface of the mat.

Applicators

The dyes can be applied with either a stencil brush or a spray. A stencil brush needs to be round with a flat, cut surface. If it is too big it will hold too much dye and this may run under the stencil. A different effect can be created by spraying the dye using a diffuser or an airbrush. A mouth diffuser is a simple piece of equipment which can be inserted in a pot of dye, then blown through to produce a fine mist of dye. An airbrush is an expensive piece of equipment, but is ideal for this.

19a, Cushions (serti, pongée 10)   19b. Cards (various techniques)

20. Daisies (false batik, 80 × 80 cm)

Fig. 107 Negative stencil

Fig. 108 Positive stencil

Choosing your design

When choosing your design, keep your stencil pattern simple to begin with as it is difficult to cut very intricate patterns even with a sharp knife. When a shape is cut from a stencil it must be attached to the outside or it will fall out. It can be attached by leaving a linking bridge to the outside of the stencil.

Stencils can be negative or positive. A positive stencil is when the actual shape and design has been cut away. After stencilling or spraying the masked background will remain undyed and the cut-out shape will be dyed. In a negative stencil, the background is cut away. After spraying the masked shape or design will remain undyed and the cut-away background will be dyed.

Cutting the stencil

Draw or trace your design on to the stencil sheet using a black marker-pen. Before cutting make sure you have a wooden board or cutting mat under your stencil sheet. Tape the stencil sheet to the mat, then begin to cut. Hold the stencil sheet firmly with one hand, making sure your fingers are well away from the path of the cutting knife. Do not angle the blade, but keep it upright when following the lines. On thicker stencil paper do not attempt to cut right through in one go. Cut lightly at first and then go back and recut your lines. When cutting rounded shapes such as circles and flowers, untape the stencil sheet and cut firmly a little at a time, moving the stencil after each cut.

Fig. 109 Stencil being cut

Application of dye

Once the stencils have been cut, a decision must be made as to which technique, stencilling or spraying, is to be used. The preparation of the work-surface, silk and dyes are different for these techniques. Stencilling is ideal for small repeat motifs, whereas spraying is effective on larger projects.

Stencilling

Prepare the work-surface for stencilling by covering it with several layers of absorbent paper. When using very fine silk, use blotting paper for extra absorption. Stretch out the silk and tape firmly to the work-surface.

Fasten the stencil to the silk with masking tape, double-sided tape, sticky tape or pins.

Prepare the dyes for use. They must be thickened into a paste-like substance so that they do not run through the silk. Epaississant or dye-thickener is used for this (see p. 95). Load the stencil brush with the paste, taking care to wipe off the excess. Hold the brush in an upright position and dab the silk through the stencil. Stencils are very effective when painted in one colour, but it is possible to experiment with different colours and shading.

If your design has more than one colour and the coloured areas are well spaced, you can paint both colours on one stencil. If the coloured areas are too close, mask out the second colour with masking tape and complete one colour first. Before you begin the second colour you must let the first colour dry completely.

Fig. 110 Thickened dye being applied

Spraying

For the spraying technique, the silk must first be treated. Stretch the silk on a frame and coat with anti-spread (antifusant). When it is dry, attach the stencil to the silk using double-sided tape and masking tape. It is advisable to stand the frame against a wall when spraying. Remember to protect the surrounding areas. Using the diffuser, air-spray or air-brush spray the dye on to the stencil. Repeat this process several times, waiting for the dye to dry in between each spraying. The spray should be about 10 cm away from the silk. Several coats of fine spray produce better results than one heavy spray.

If your design has more than one colour it is necessary to cut as many stencils as colours required. When using two stencils, it is important to line them up before spraying. One method is to place the stencils on top of each other and use a hole punch to make a neat hole in each corner. Remember to mask this before spraying. Multi-coloured designs can be achieved using a single stencil by removing the stencil and changing its position between each spraying.

Fig. 111 Spraying the dye

Fig. 112 Overlapping stencil pattern

Faults that may occur

The paint may have run under the stencil.
This may have been caused by the paint
being too runny, the brush being overloaded
with dye or, if spraying, holding the air-
spray too close to the fabric. It is impossible
to remove these stains, so they would need to
be camouflaged by overprinting.

**Reprinting may have occurred due to a dirty
stencil.** Ensure that the underside of the
stencil has been wiped clean and is dry before
replacing on the silk. If the second stencil
overlaps the first, make sure that the first
colour is dry before applying the second.

Fig. 113 Overlapping
stencil pattern

Part three
Ideas & examples

This section shows completed projects using the various techniques described in this book. Silk painting can be used to create many different articles, some of which are shown in this section.

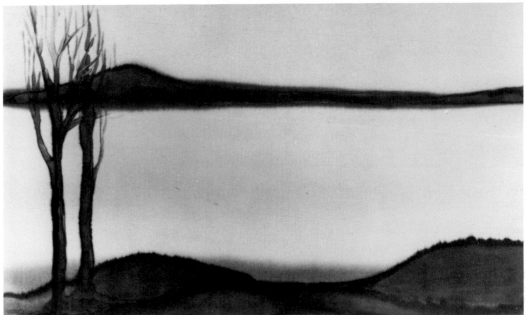

Fig. 114 *Naif houses*
(40 cm × 50 cm pongée 9)
Serti technique with
grey gutta and a wash
background

Fig. 115 *Blue Lake*
(30 cm × 40 cm pongée
9) Watercolour and
epaississant techniques

Fig. 116 *Landscape*
(40 cm × 50 cm pongée 9)
Wax, salt and
watercolour techniques

Fig. 117 *Pansies*
(45 cm × 50 cm pongée 9)
Wax and watercolour
techniques

Fig. 118 *Scarves*
(90 cm × 90 cm pongée 9)
Serti and wax
techniques. Hand-rolled
hems

Fig. 119 *Ties* (Wild silk) Watercolour and salt techniques

Fig. 120 *T-shirt* (Crêpe de chine) Appliqued butterfly using serti technique

Fig. 121 *Striped and flowered T-shirt* (pongée, cloqué. Flowers, anti-spread, pongée 9)

Fig. 122 *Jumper*
(Angora, crêpe de chine)
Butterfly motifs appliqued
to angora jumper (knitted
by Emer Leydon)

Fig. 123 *Cushions*
(40 cm × 40 cm
pongée 10) Serti and
salt techniques

Fig. 124 *Lampshade*
(Pongée 9) Serti
technique with gold
gutta

Suppliers

Britain

Silk

Pongées Ltd, 184–186 Old St, London
  EC1V 9BP
Wm. H. Bennett & Sons Ltd,
  Crown Royal Park, Higher Hillgate,
  Stockport SK1 3HB
Dryad, PO Box 38, Northgates, Leicester
  LE1 9BU
E. J. Arnold & Son Ltd, Parkside Lane,
  Dewsbury Rd, Leeds LS11 5TD
Versatile Silks, 23 Pensham Hill, Pershore,
  Worcestershire

Dyes and Equipment

Candle Makers Suppliers, 28 Blythe Rd,
  London W14 0HA
Atlantis Paper Company Ltd, Gullivers
  Warf, 105 Wapping Lane, London
  E1 9RW
L. Cornellissen & Son Ltd,
  22 Great Queen St, Covent Garden,
  London WC2B 5BH
Dryad, PO Box 38, Northgates, Leicester
  LE1 9BU
E. J. Arnold & Son Ltd, Parkside Lane,
  Dewsbury Rd, Leeds LS11 5TD

Europe

Silk Dyes and Equipment

Sennelier, rue du Moulin-à-Cailloux, Orly,
  Senia 40894567, France

R. Leprince, 19 rue de Cléry, 75002, Paris,
  France
Ponsard Frères, 28 rue du Sentier, 75002,
  Paris, France
Pébéo, Usine St Marcel, 13367, Marseille,
  France
Dupont, route de Guindreef, 44600
  Saint·Nazaire, France
La Fourmi, 236 rue Vanderkindere 236,
  1180 Brussels, Belgium
Passe Temps, 292 avenue Georges Henri,
  1200 Brussels, Belgium
Le Folio, Parvis St Henri 56, 1200
  Brussels, Belgium
Galerie Smend, Mainzer Strasse 28,
  Postfach 250450, D-5001 Köln 1,
  West Germany
Hobbidee, Turbinstrasse 7, 7000
  Stuttgart 31, West Germany

If readers have difficulty in obtaining the
materials and equipment mentioned in
this book, silk painting kits and further
information are available from:
Beaver Crafts, Threepenny Cottage,
  Quarley, Andover, Hants SP11 8P2

Further reading

Ferenc Pinter & Donatella Volpi *A Guide To Drawing* Dryad
Michael Woods *Starting Pencil Drawing* Dryad
    Starting Life Drawing Dryad
    Perspective in Art Batsford
Wilfrid Ball *Sketching for Landscapes* Dryad
Monique Levi-Strauss *The Cashmere Shawl* Dryad
Arthur Baker *The Calligraphy Manual* Dryad
John Lancaster *Basic Penmanship* Dryad
Angus Scott *Drawing in Pen and Ink* Batsford
Gwen White *Perspective* Batsford
Christopher Jarman *Illumination* Dryad
Heather Schofield *Flower Painting Techniques* Batsford
Joyce Hargreaves *The Techniques of Hand Print Making* Batsford
E. H. Gombrich *Art and Illusion* Phaidon Press
Wilhelm von Bode & Ernst Kuhmel *Antique Rugs from the Near East* Bell & Hyman
Ken Ponting *A Dictionary of Dyes and Dyeing* Bell & Hyman
David Talbot Rice *The Art of Byzantium* Thames & Hudson

Index